TUNDRA

Published by Willow Creek Press, Inc.
P.O. Box 147, Minocqua, Wisconsin 54548

Printed in China

TUNDRA
NOTHING BUT SNOWMEN

CHAD CARPENTER

WILLOW CREEK PRESS®

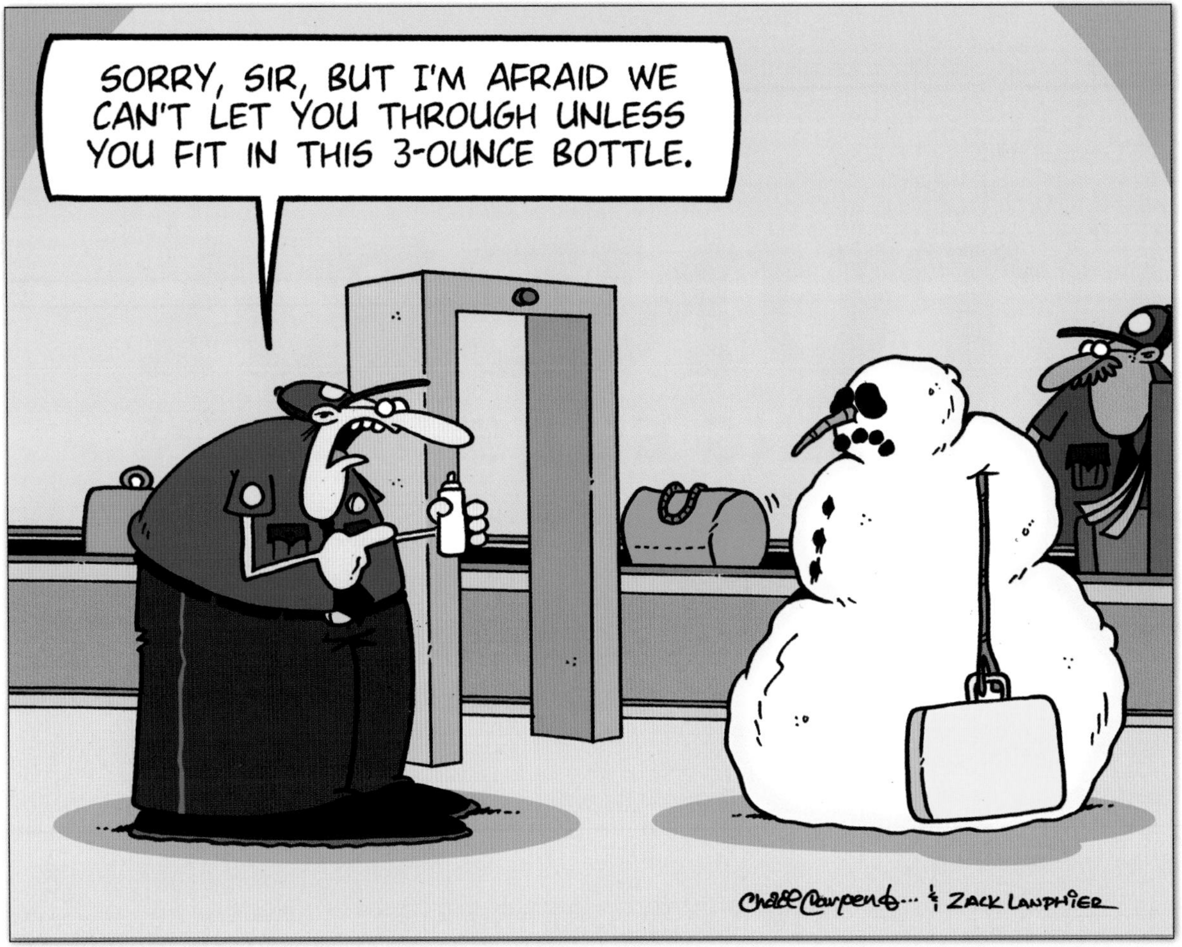
SORRY, SIR, BUT I'M AFRAID WE CAN'T LET YOU THROUGH UNLESS YOU FIT IN THIS 3-OUNCE BOTTLE.
ZACK LANPHIER

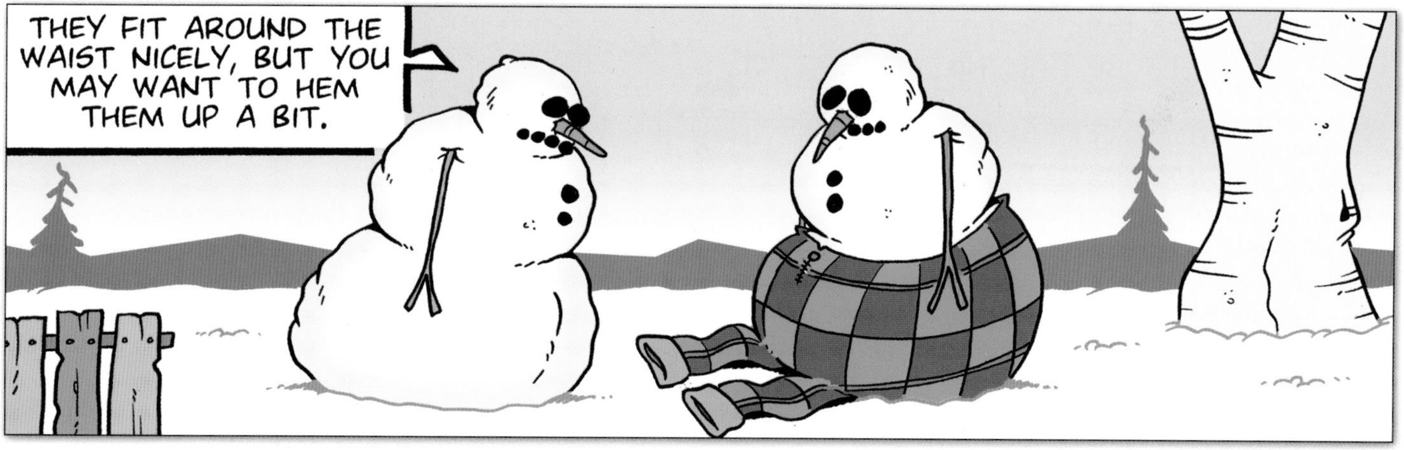
THEY FIT AROUND THE WAIST NICELY, BUT YOU MAY WANT TO HEM THEM UP A BIT.

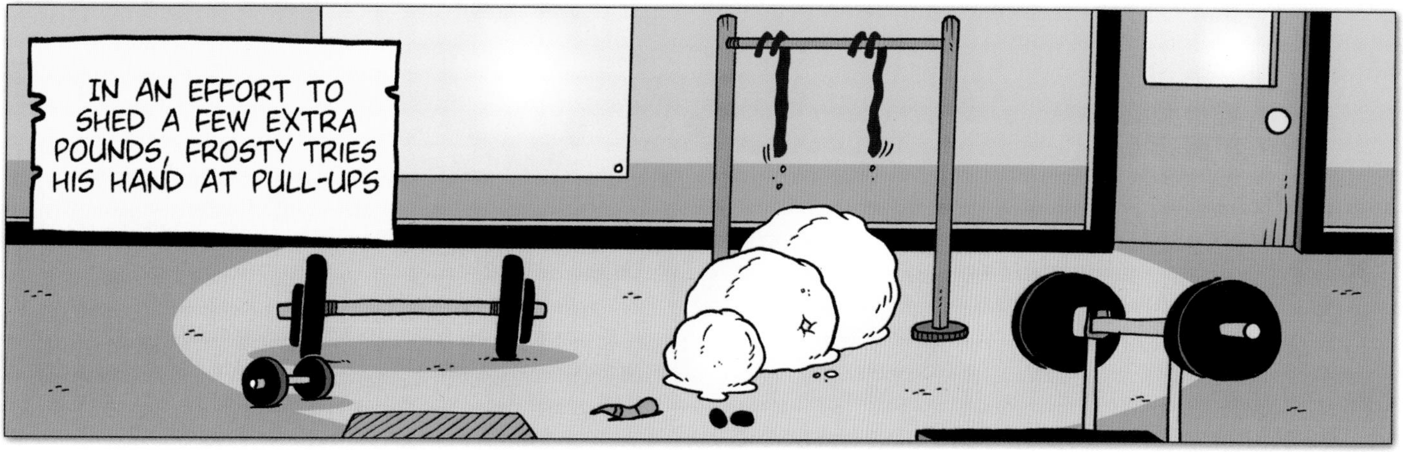
IN AN EFFORT TO SHED A FEW EXTRA POUNDS, FROSTY TRIES HIS HAND AT PULL-UPS

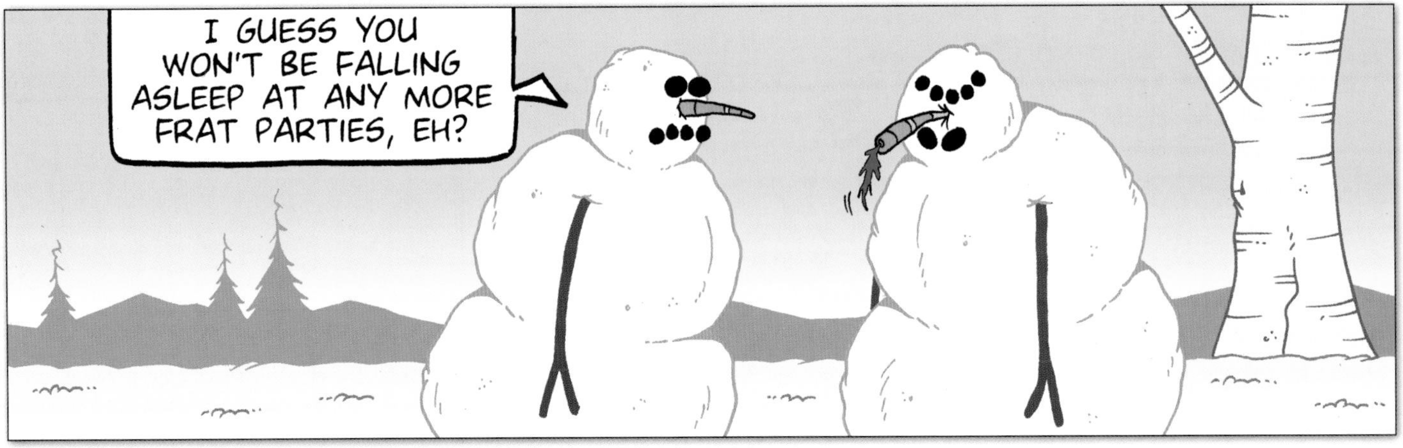
I GUESS YOU WON'T BE FALLING ASLEEP AT ANY MORE FRAT PARTIES, EH?

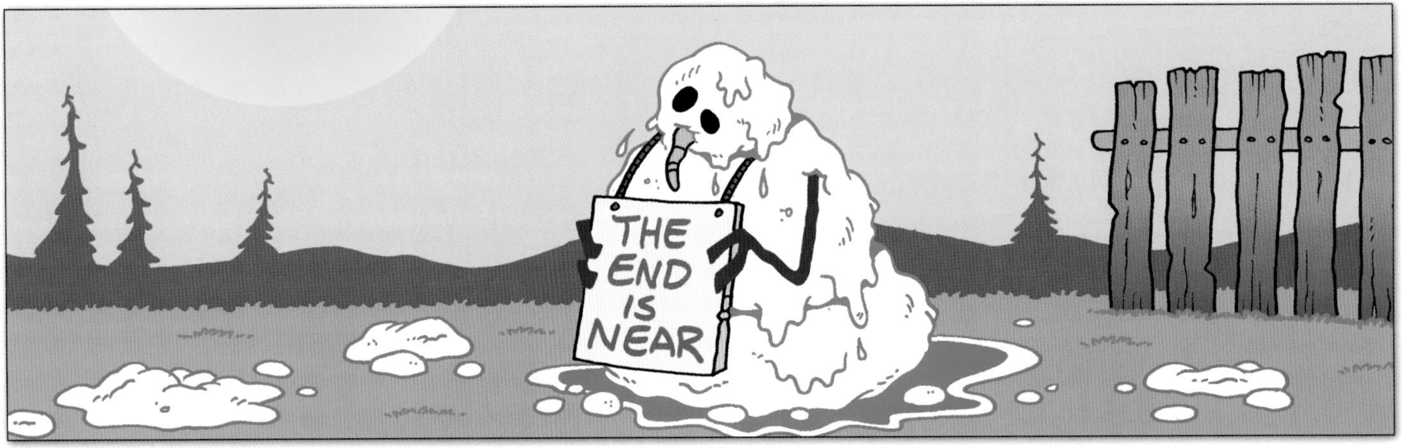
THE END IS NEAR

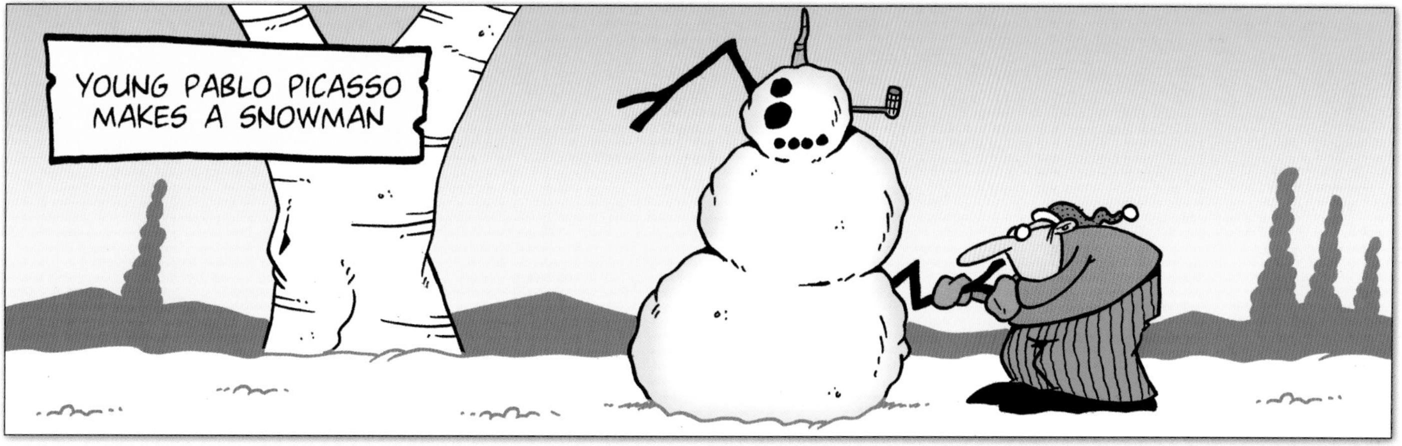
YOUNG PABLO PICASSO
MAKES A SNOWMAN

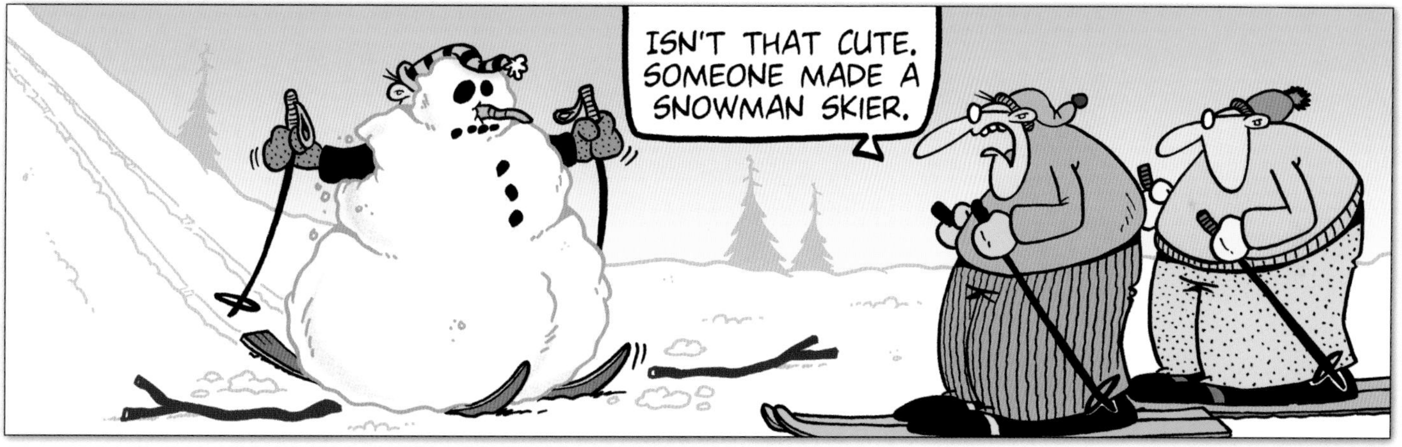
ISN'T THAT CUTE.
SOMEONE MADE A
SNOWMAN SKIER.

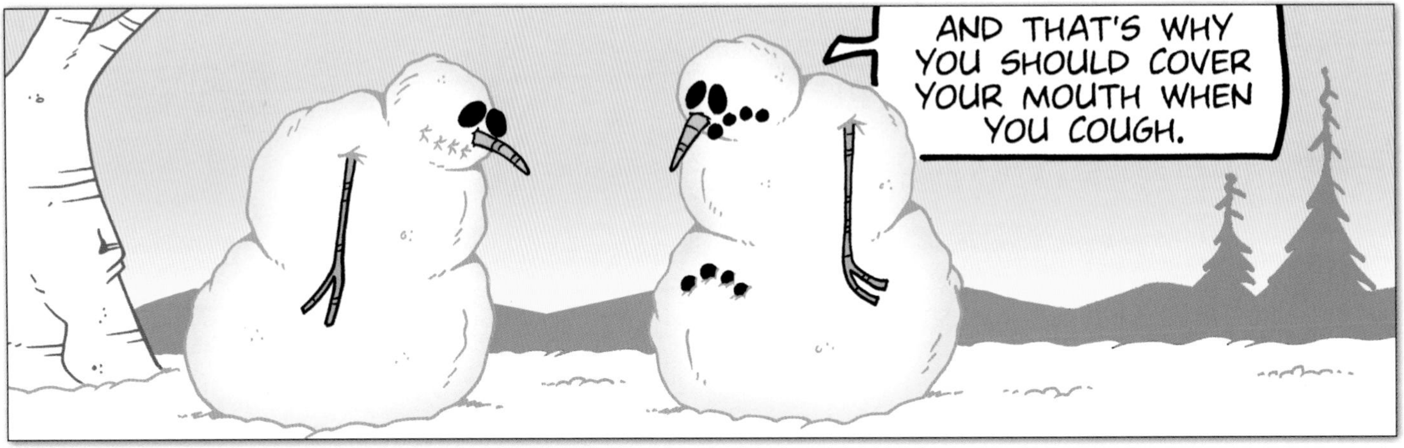
AND THAT'S WHY YOU SHOULD COVER YOUR MOUTH WHEN YOU COUGH.

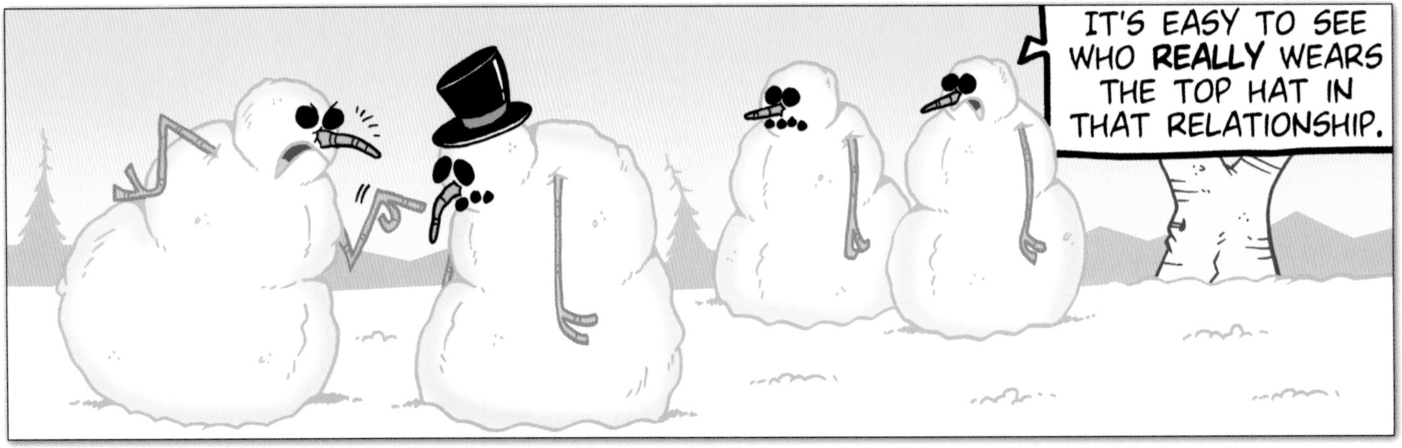
IT'S EASY TO SEE WHO **REALLY** WEARS THE TOP HAT IN THAT RELATIONSHIP.

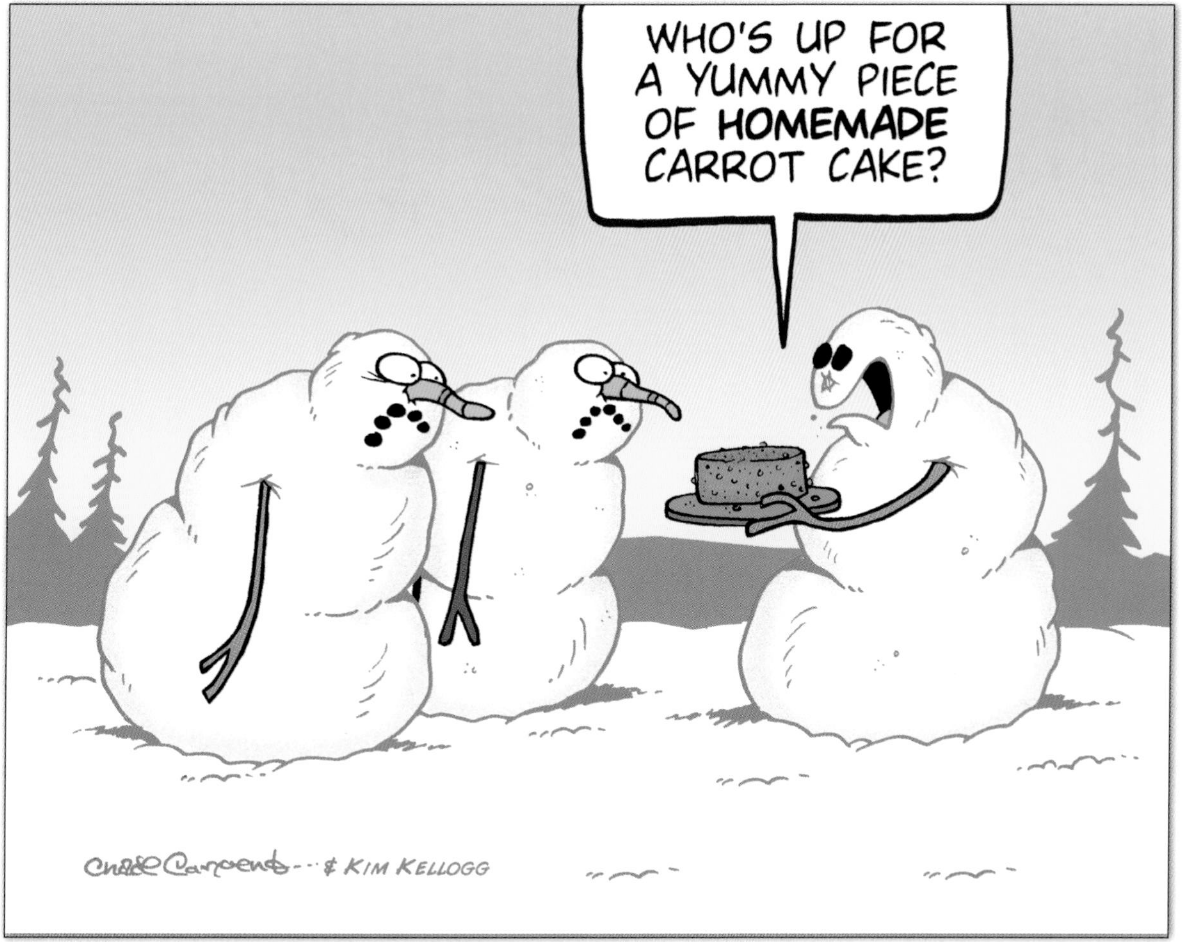
WHO'S UP FOR A YUMMY PIECE OF **HOMEMADE** CARROT CAKE?
& KIM KELLOGG

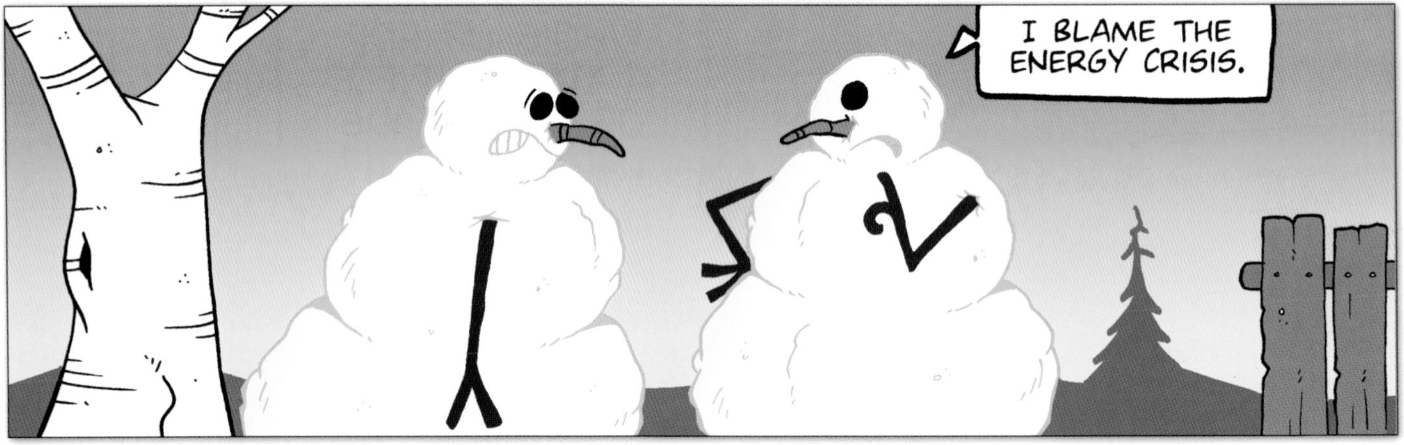
I BLAME THE ENERGY CRISIS.

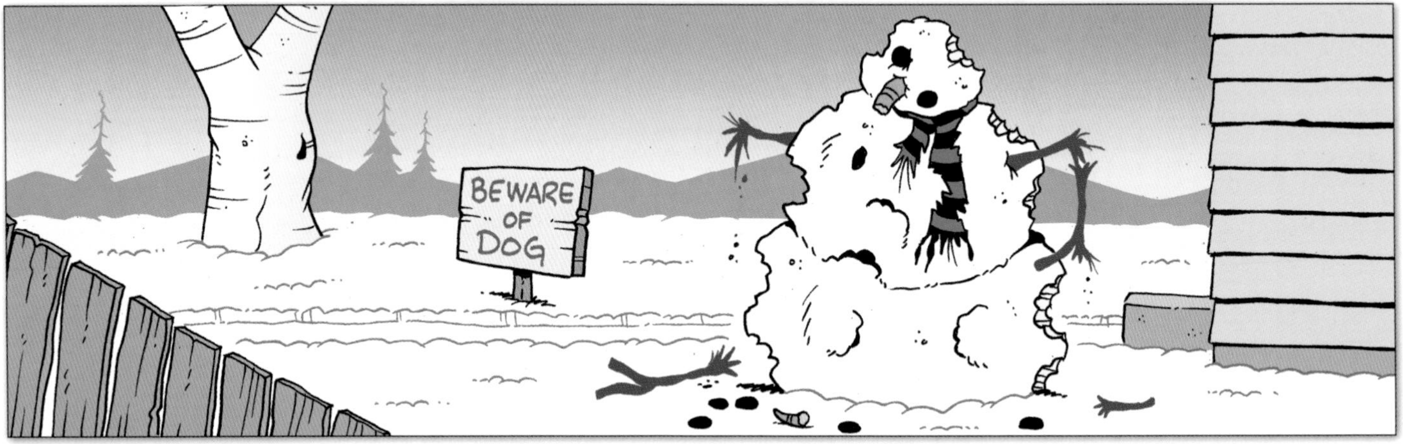
BEWARE OF DOG

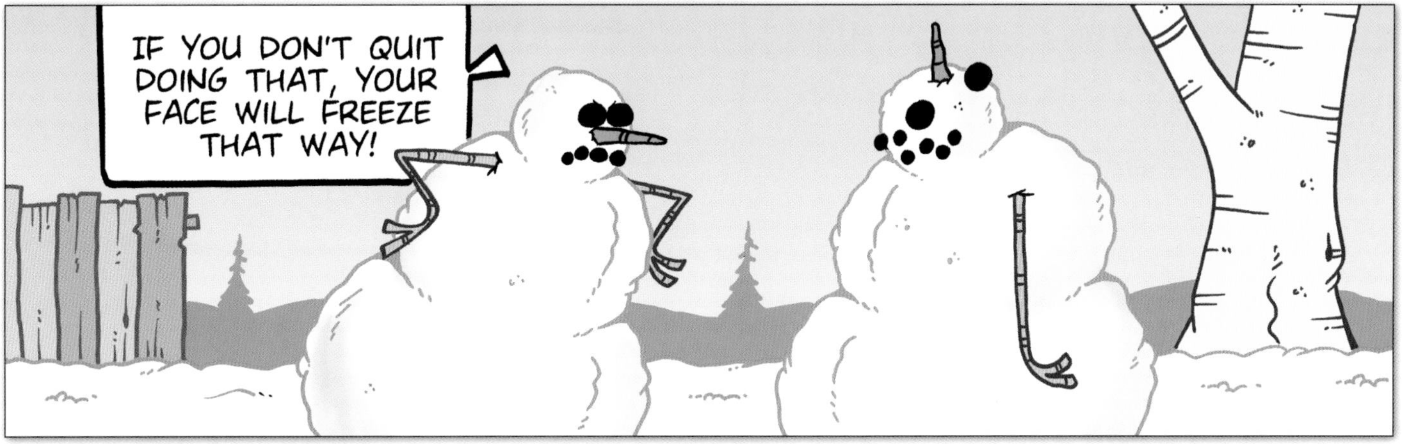
IF YOU DON'T QUIT DOING THAT, YOUR FACE WILL FREEZE THAT WAY!

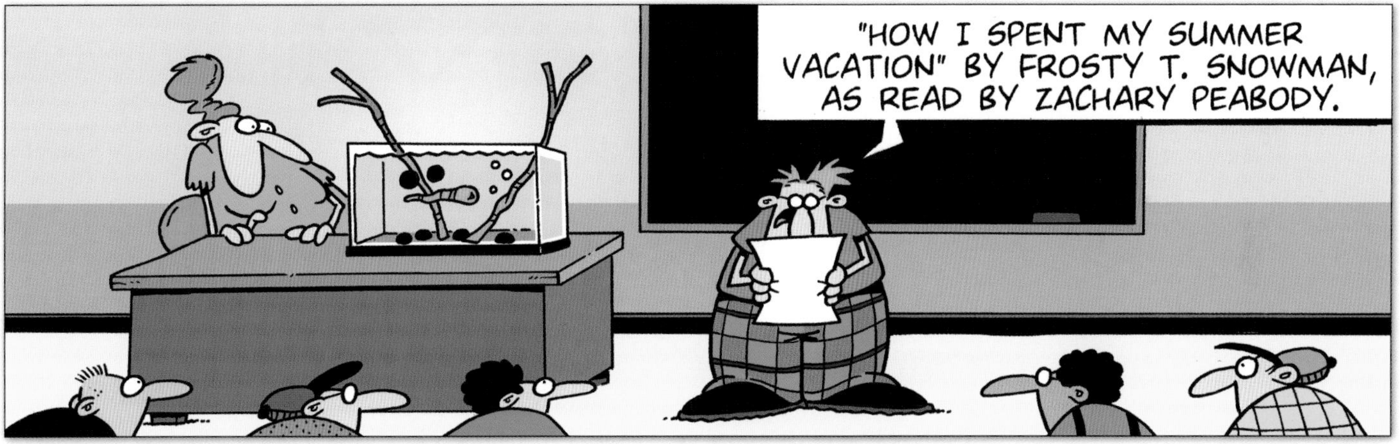
"HOW I SPENT MY SUMMER VACATION" BY FROSTY T. SNOWMAN, AS READ BY ZACHARY PEABODY.

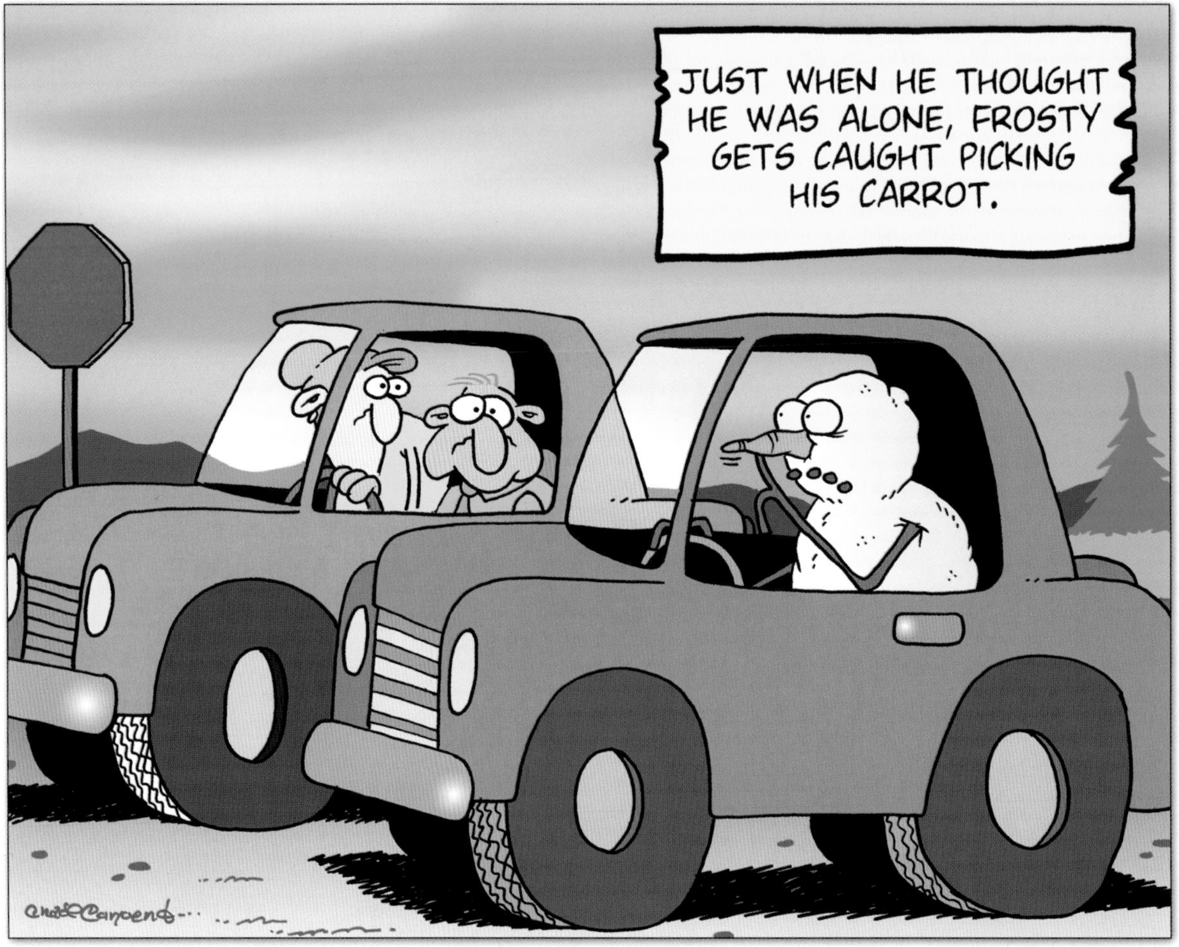
JUST WHEN HE THOUGHT HE WAS ALONE, FROSTY GETS CAUGHT PICKING HIS CARROT.

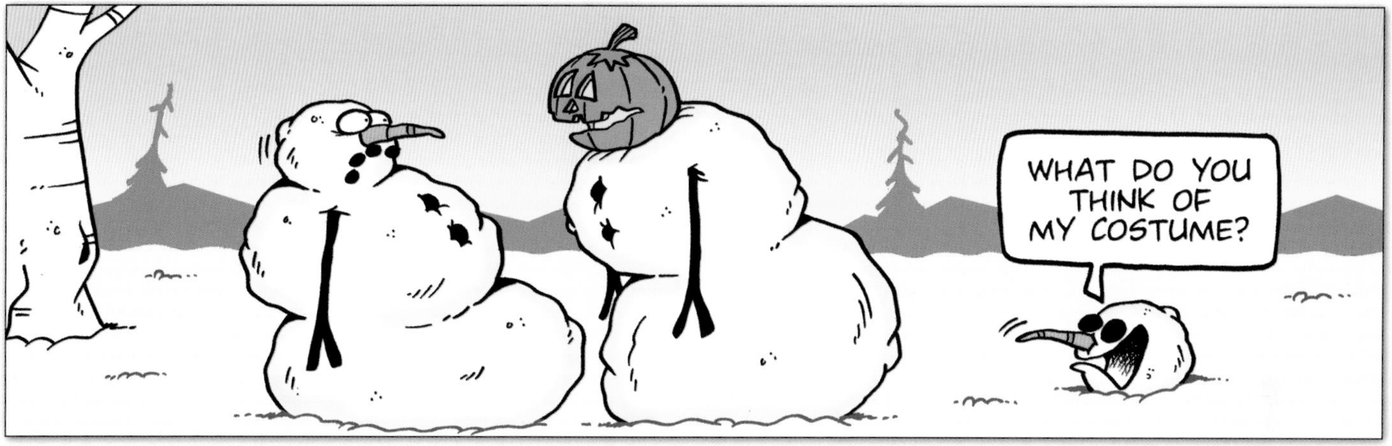
WHAT DO YOU THINK OF MY COSTUME?

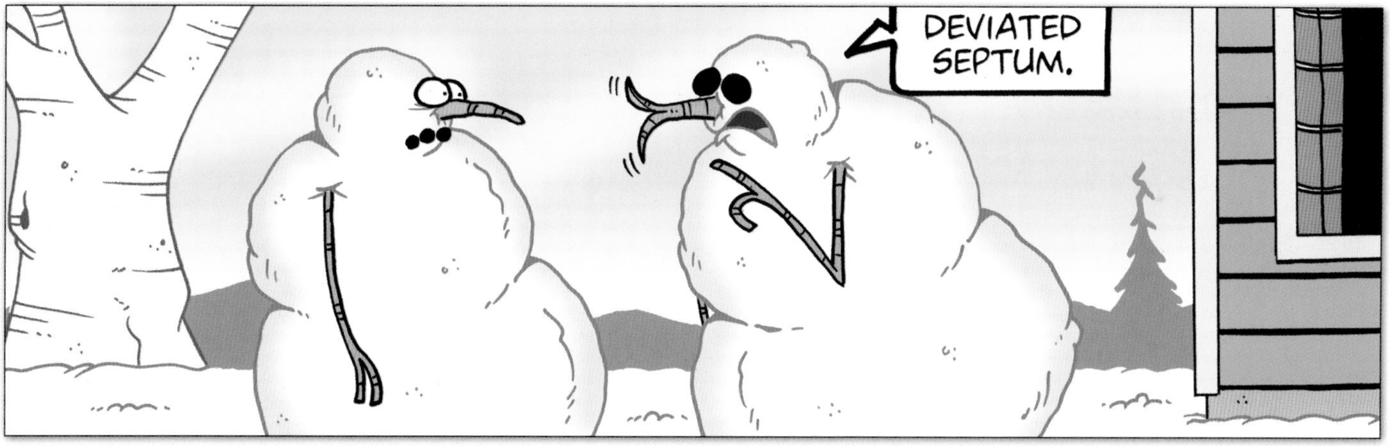
DEVIATED SEPTUM.

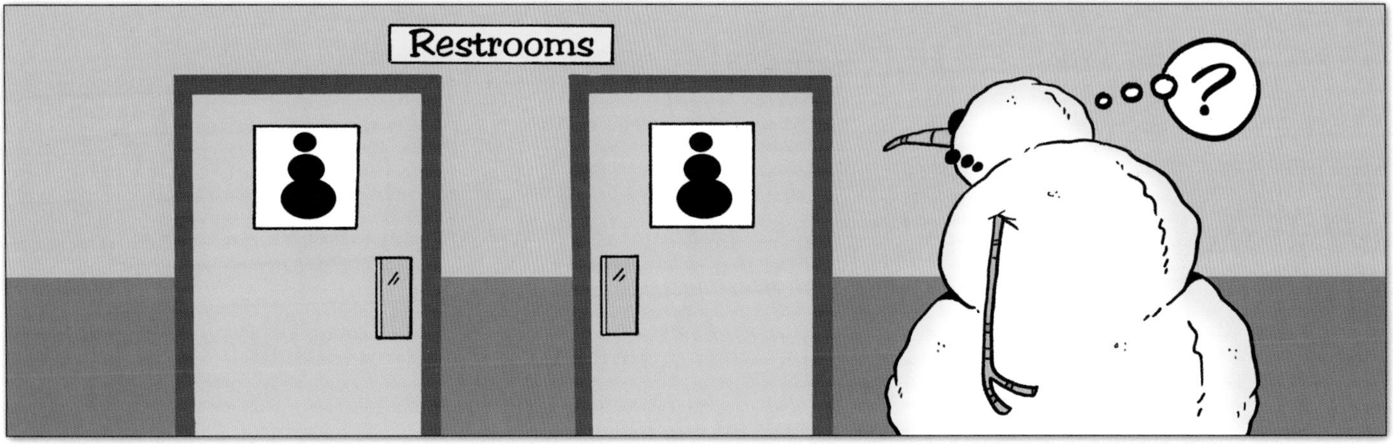
Restrooms
?

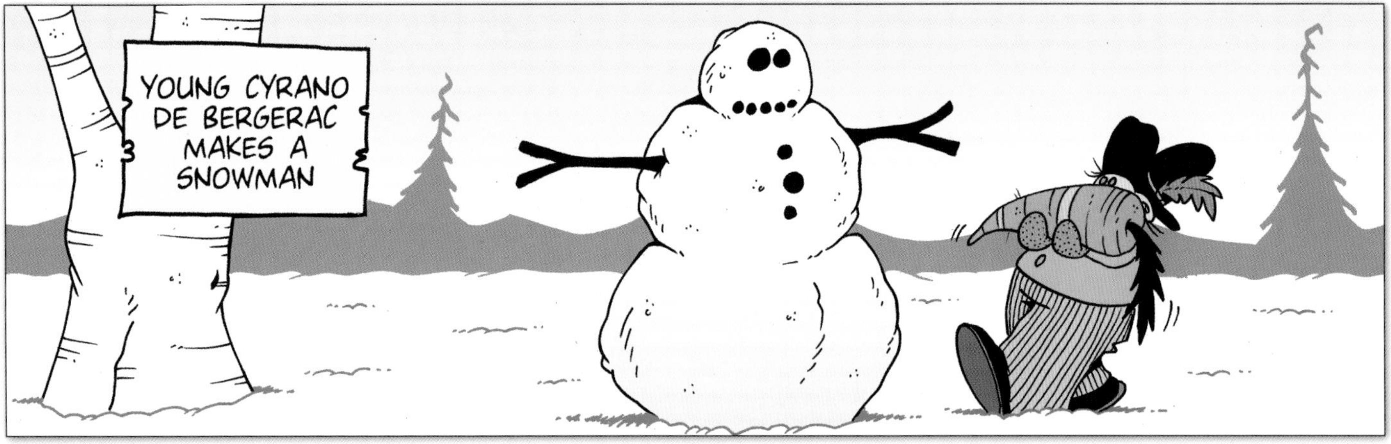
YOUNG CYRANO DE BERGERAC MAKES A SNOWMAN

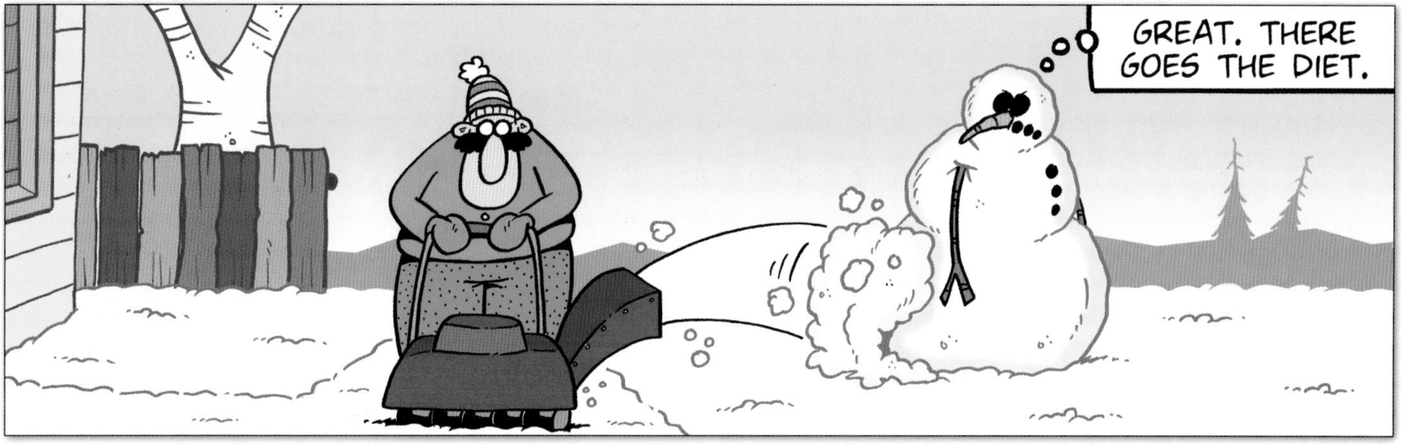
GREAT. THERE GOES THE DIET.

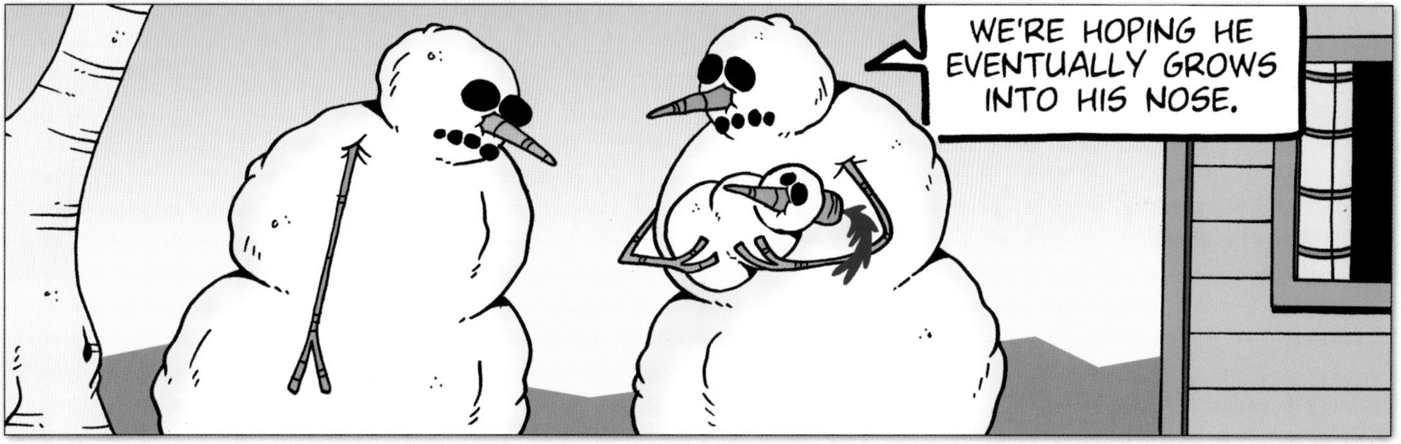
WE'RE HOPING HE EVENTUALLY GROWS INTO HIS NOSE.

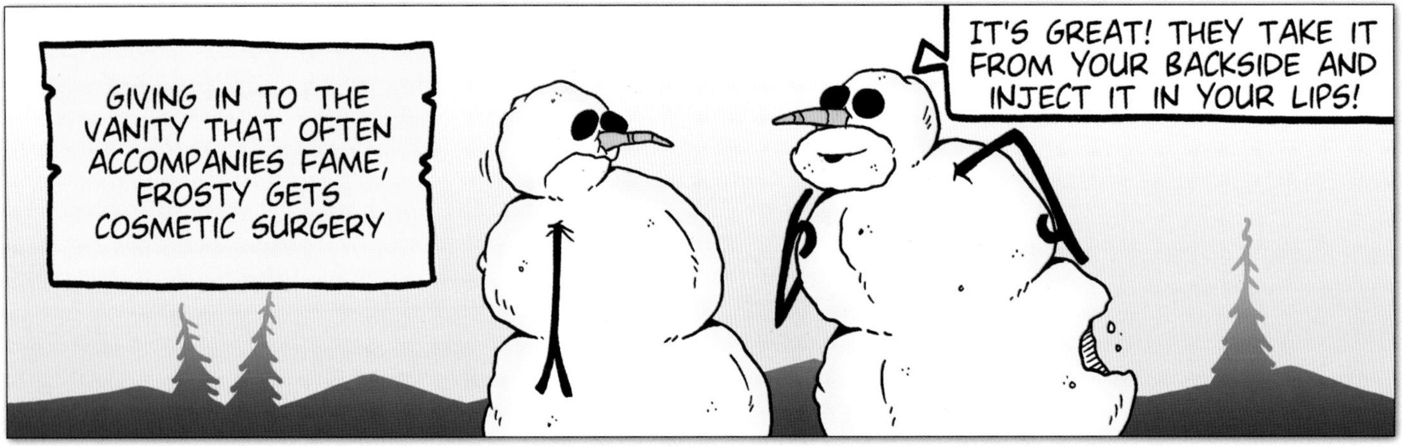
GIVING IN TO THE VANITY THAT OFTEN ACCOMPANIES FAME, FROSTY GETS COSMETIC SURGERY
IT'S GREAT! THEY TAKE IT FROM YOUR BACKSIDE AND INJECT IT IN YOUR LIPS!

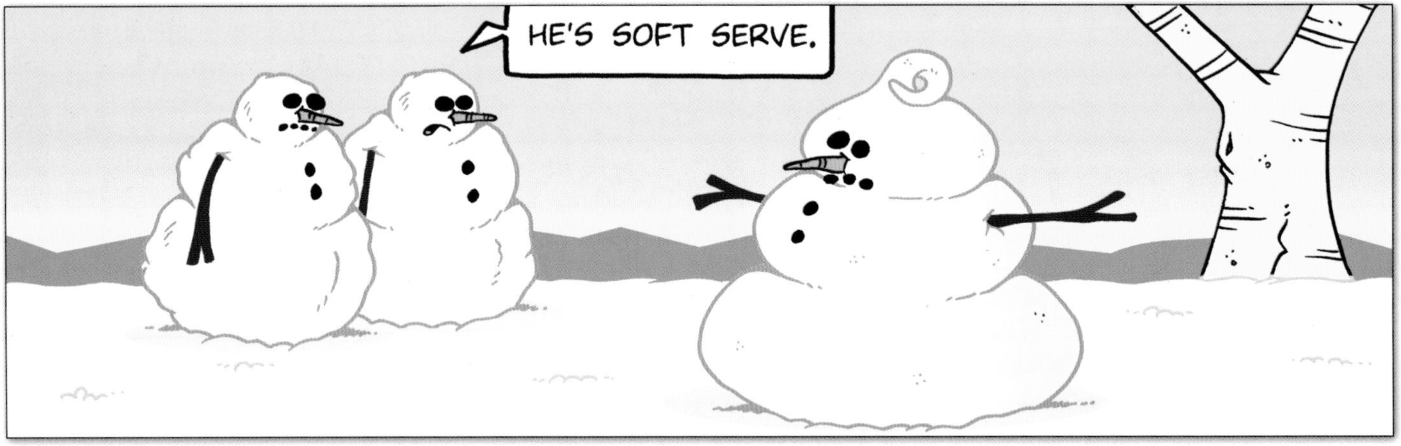
HE'S SOFT SERVE.

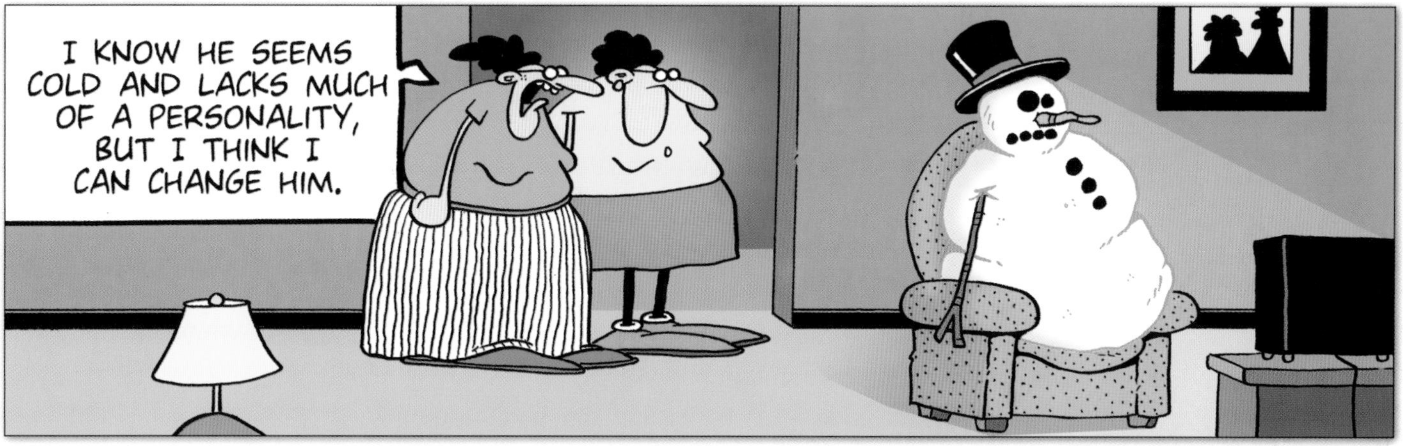
I KNOW HE SEEMS COLD AND LACKS MUCH OF A PERSONALITY, BUT I THINK I CAN CHANGE HIM.

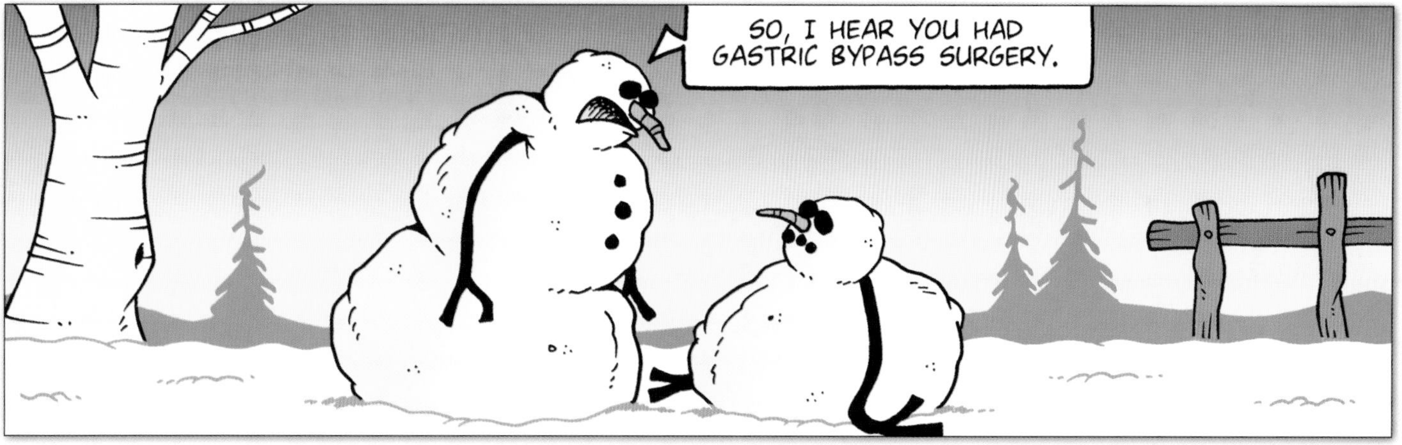
SO, I HEAR YOU HAD GASTRIC BYPASS SURGERY.

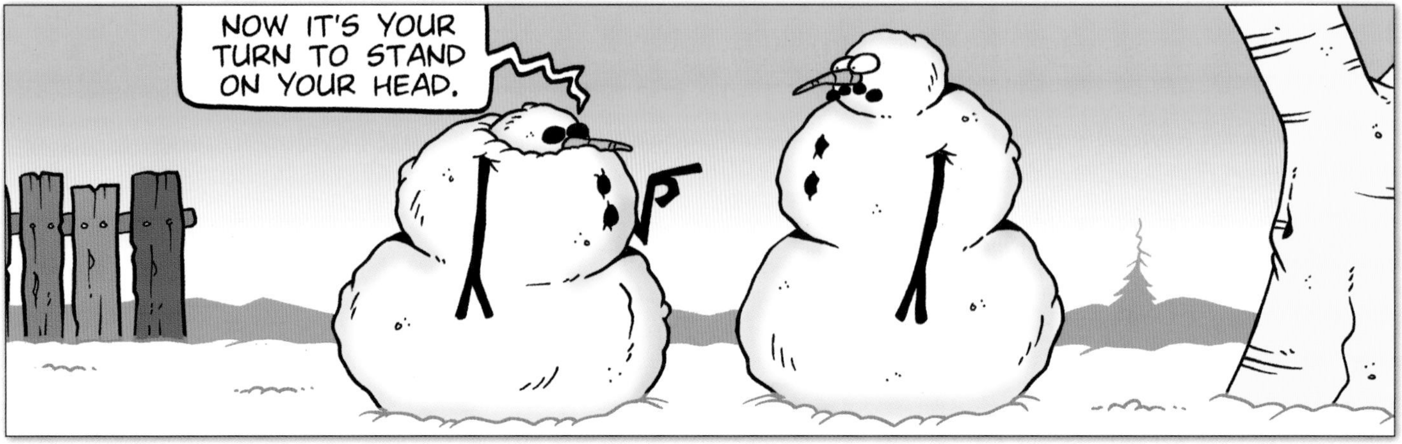
NOW IT'S YOUR TURN TO STAND ON YOUR HEAD.

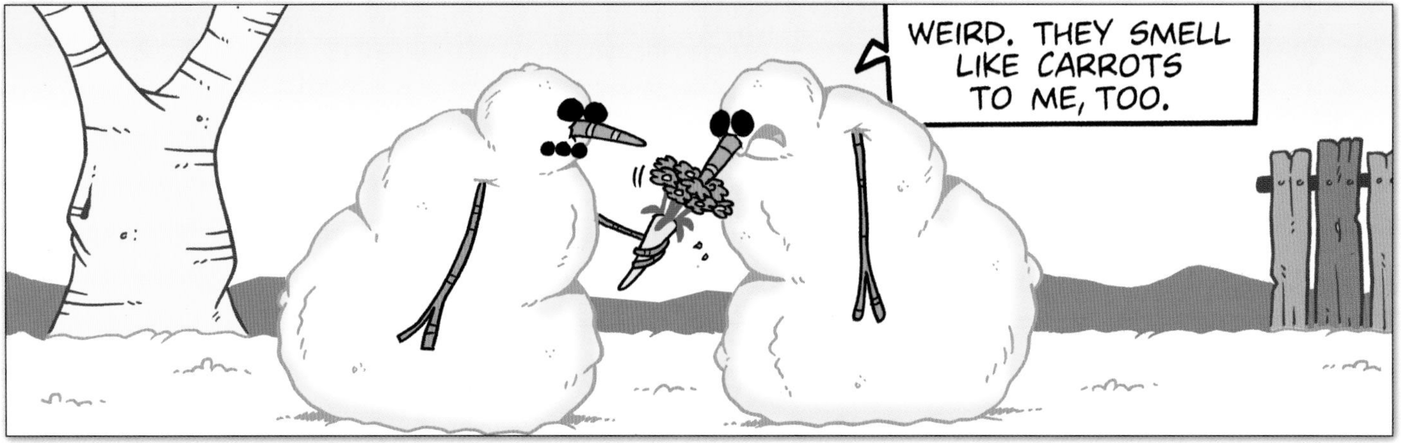
WEIRD. THEY SMELL LIKE CARROTS TO ME, TOO.

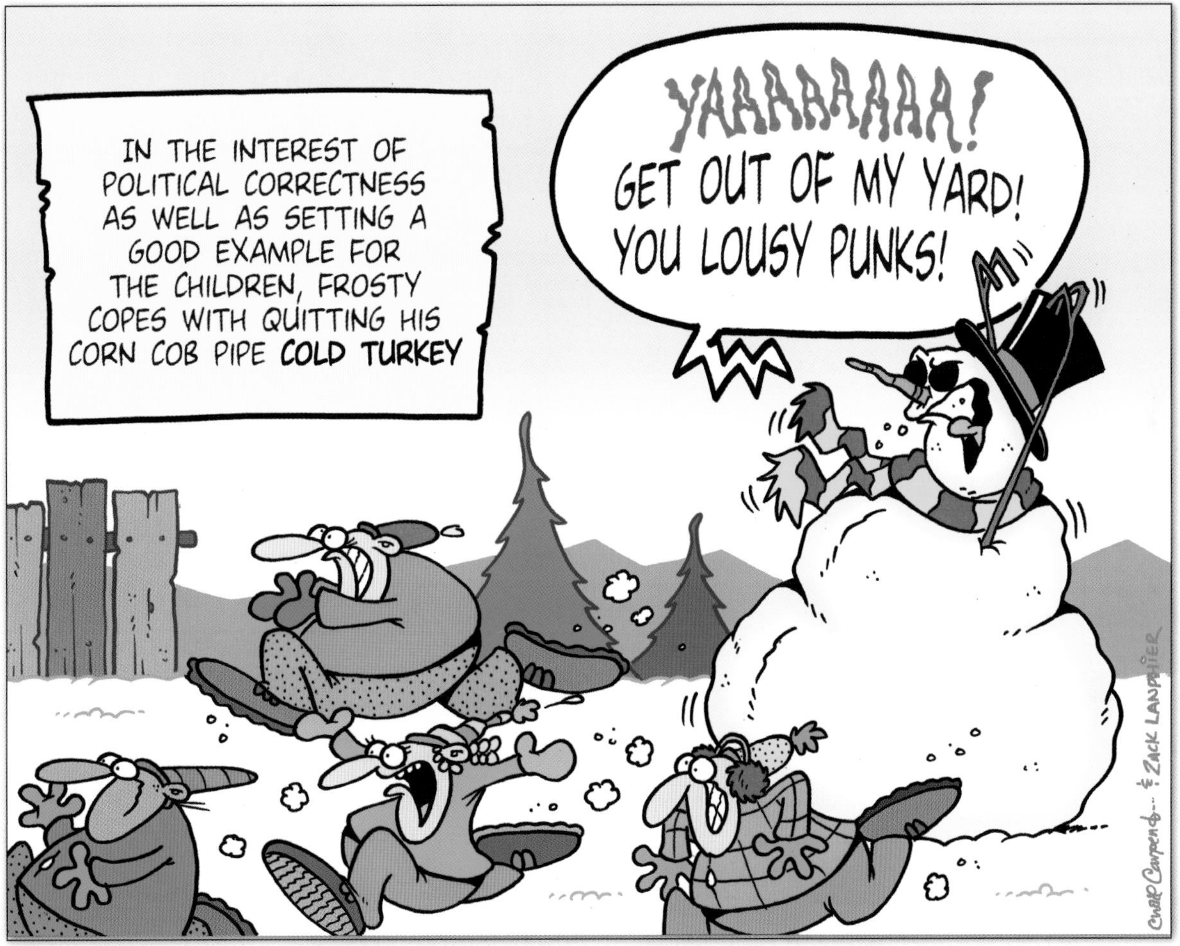
IN THE INTEREST OF POLITICAL CORRECTNESS AS WELL AS SETTING A GOOD EXAMPLE FOR THE CHILDREN, FROSTY COPES WITH QUITTING HIS CORN COB PIPE **COLD TURKEY**
YAAAAAAAA!
GET OUT OF MY YARD! YOU LOUSY PUNKS!
ZACK LANPHIER

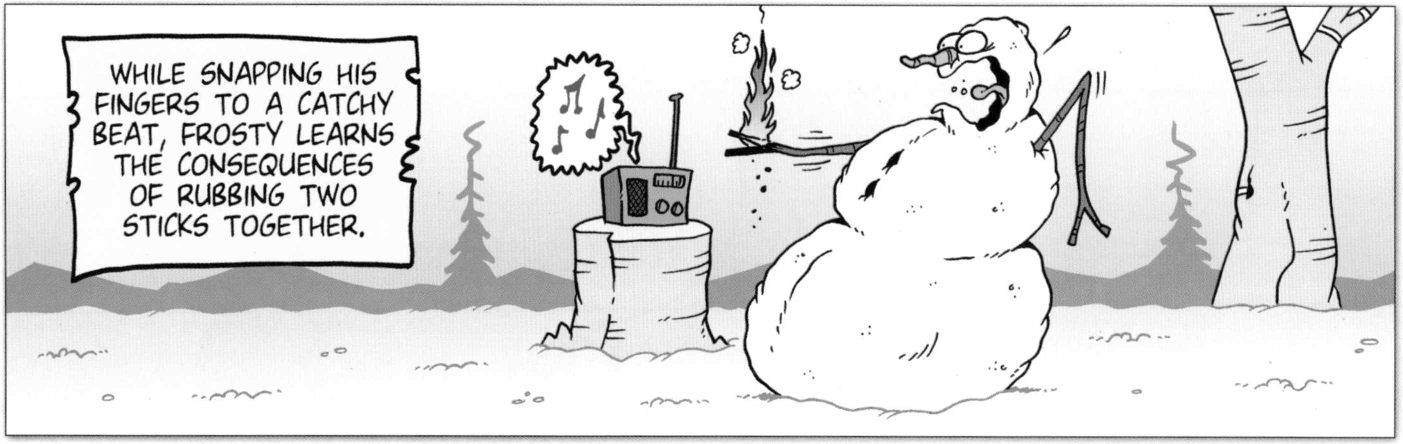
WHILE SNAPPING HIS FINGERS TO A CATCHY BEAT, FROSTY LEARNS THE CONSEQUENCES OF RUBBING TWO STICKS TOGETHER.

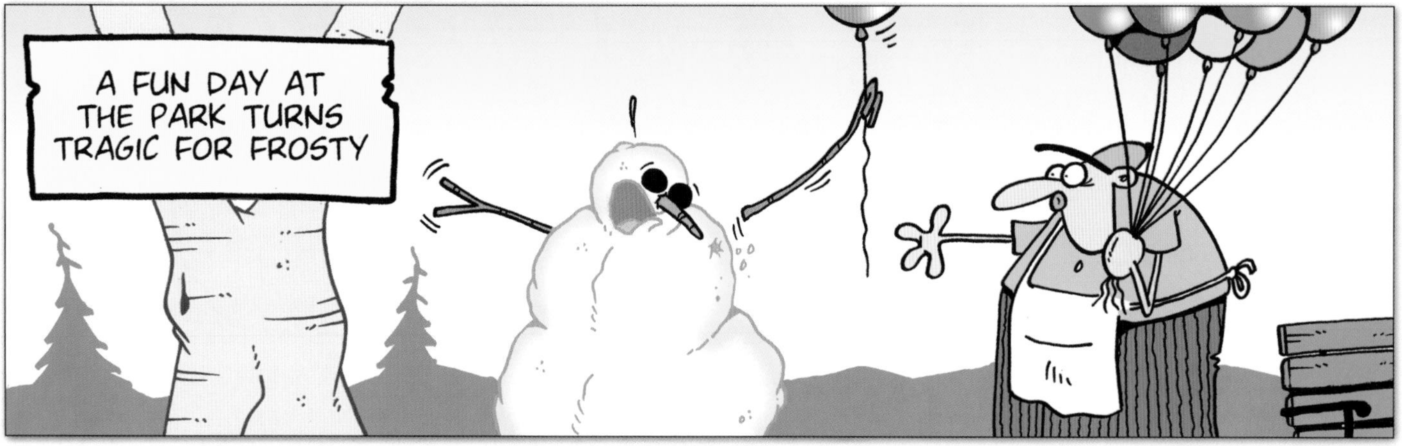
A FUN DAY AT THE PARK TURNS TRAGIC FOR FROSTY

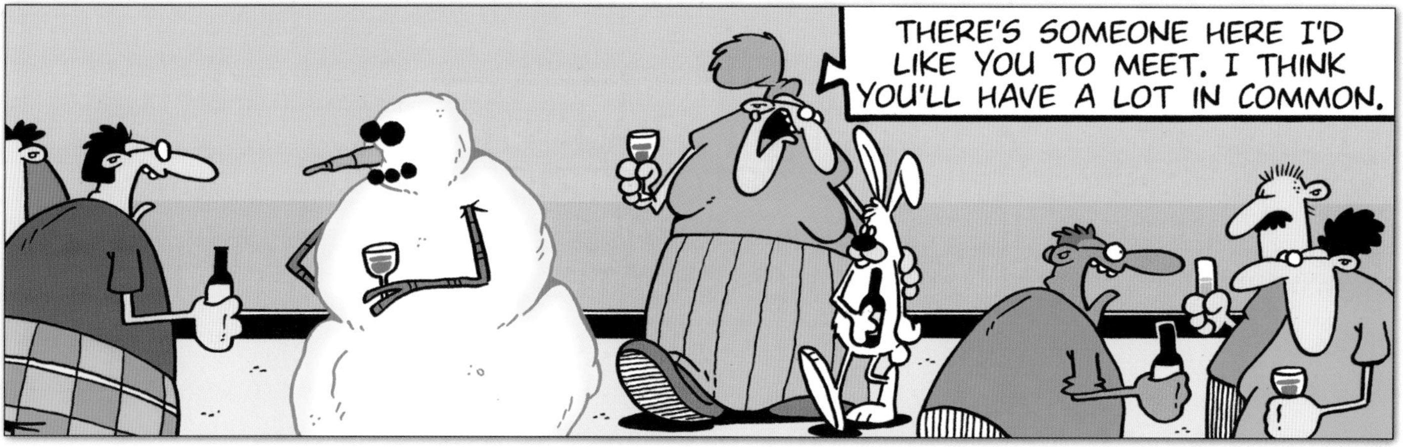
THERE'S SOMEONE HERE I'D LIKE YOU TO MEET. I THINK YOU'LL HAVE A LOT IN COMMON.

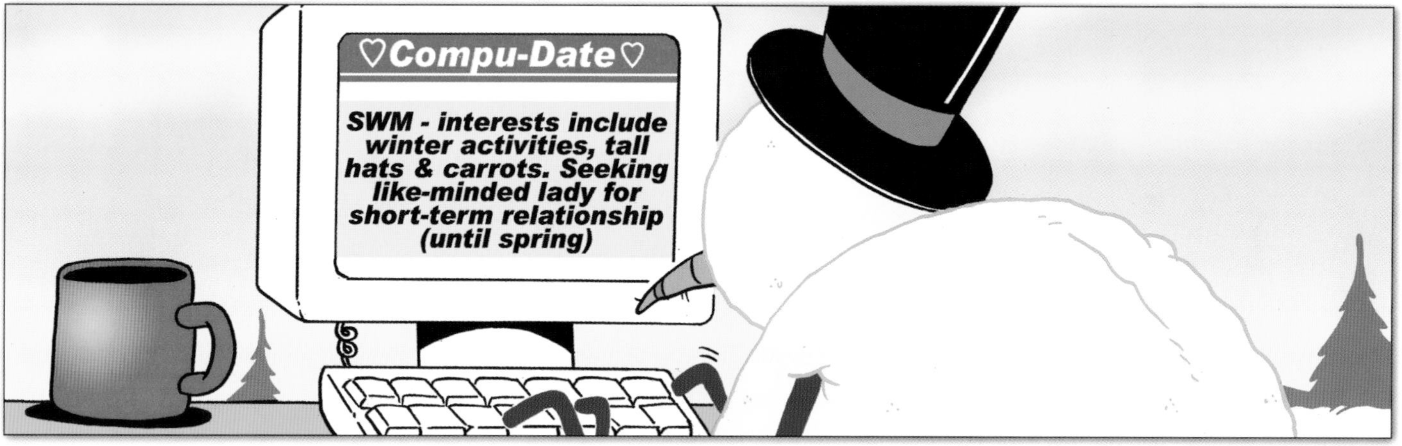
♡Compu-Date♡
SWM - interests include winter activities, tall hats & carrots. Seeking like-minded lady for short-term relationship (until spring)

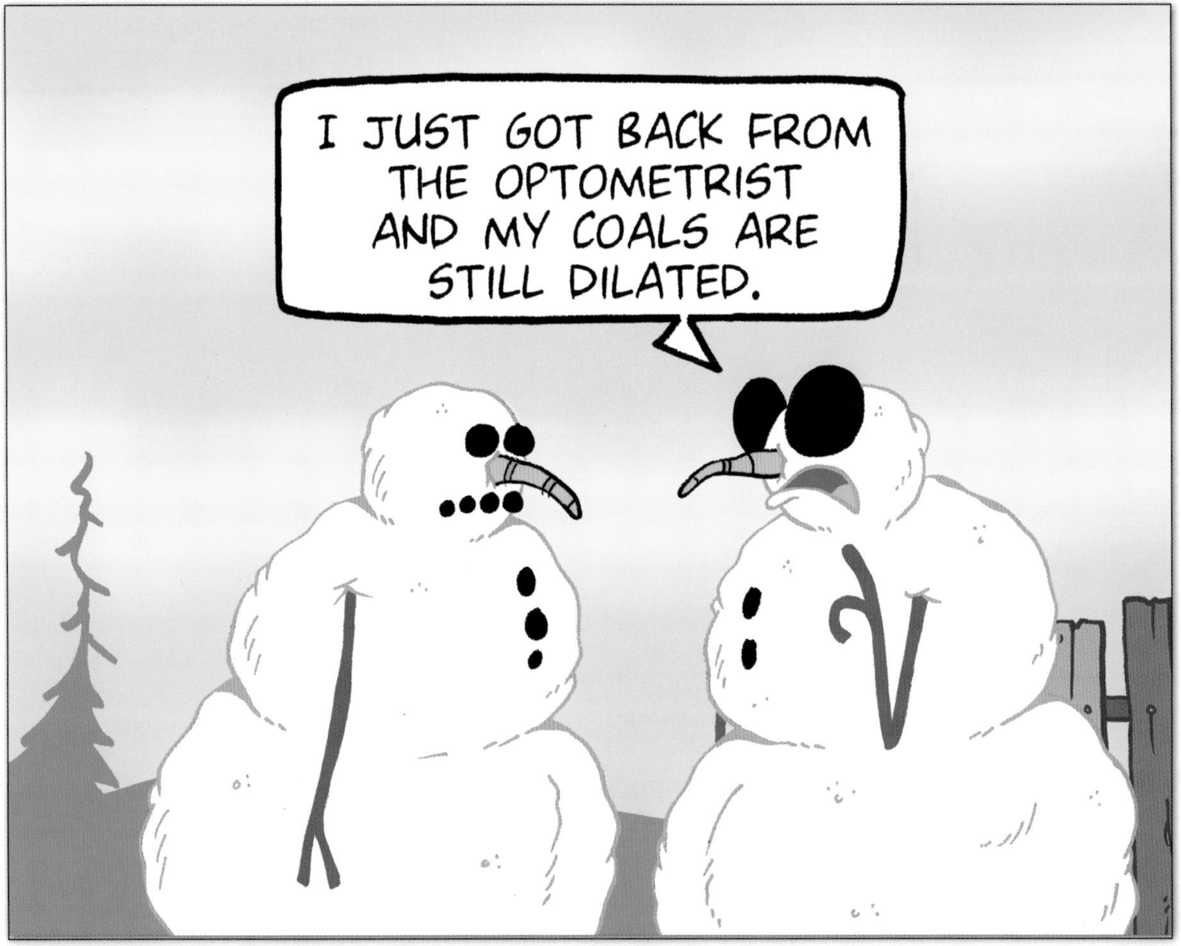
I JUST GOT BACK FROM THE OPTOMETRIST AND MY COALS ARE STILL DILATED.

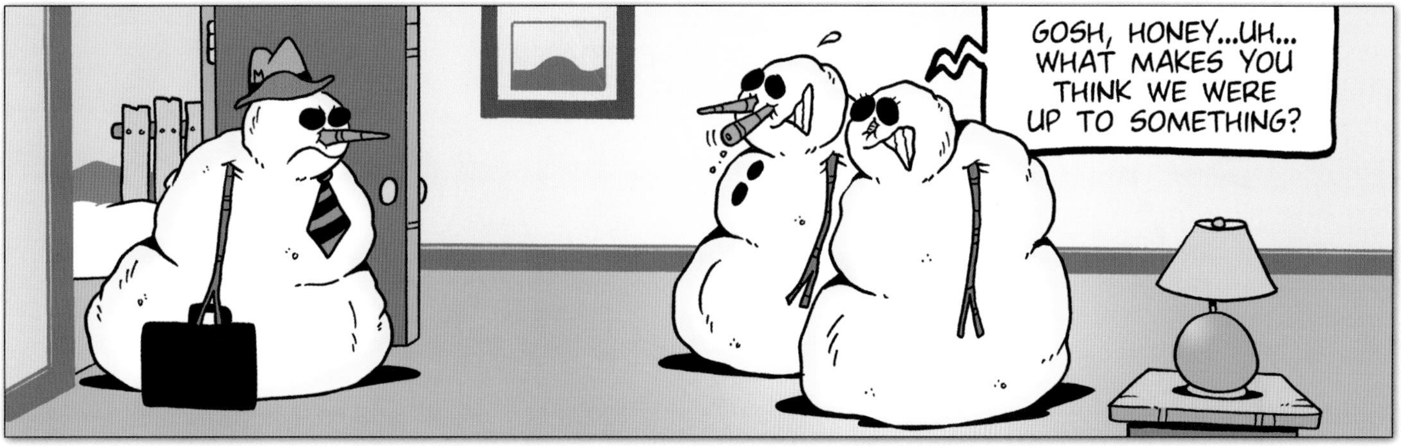
GOSH, HONEY...UH... WHAT MAKES YOU THINK WE WERE UP TO SOMETHING?

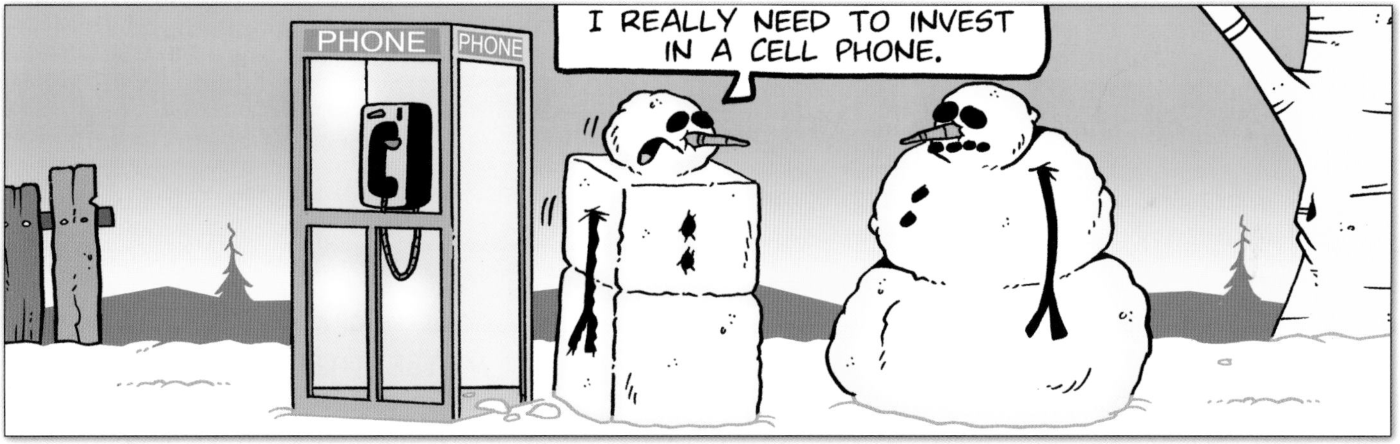
PHONE
PHONE
I REALLY NEED TO INVEST IN A CELL PHONE.

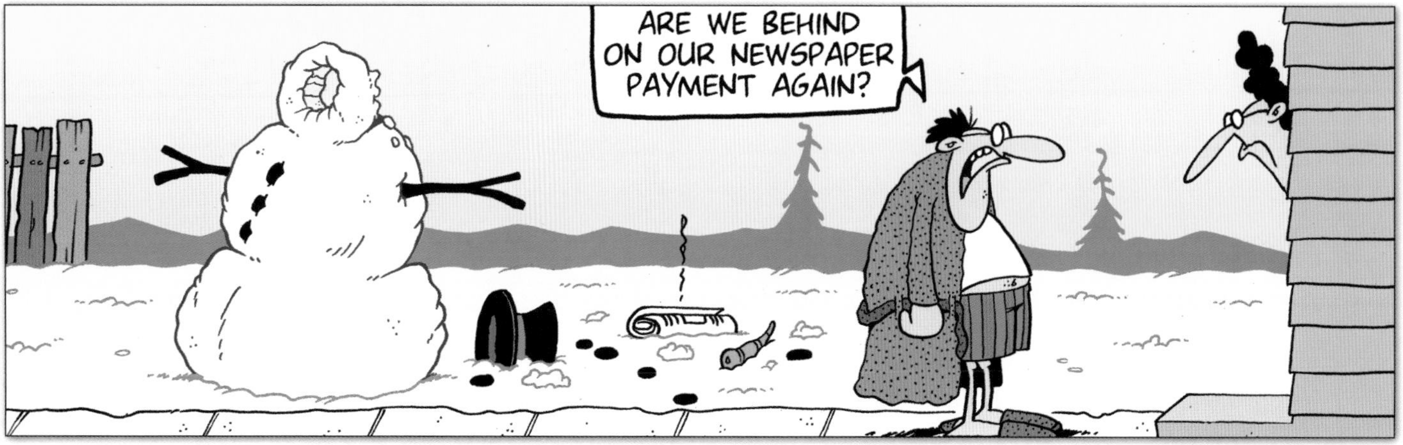
ARE WE BEHIND ON OUR NEWSPAPER PAYMENT AGAIN?

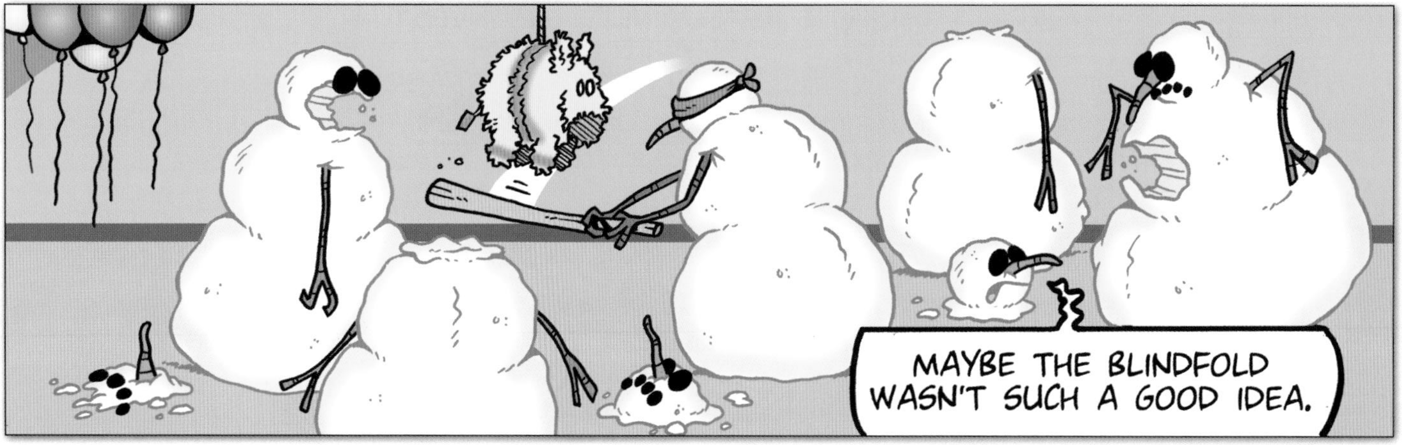
MAYBE THE BLINDFOLD WASN'T SUCH A GOOD IDEA.

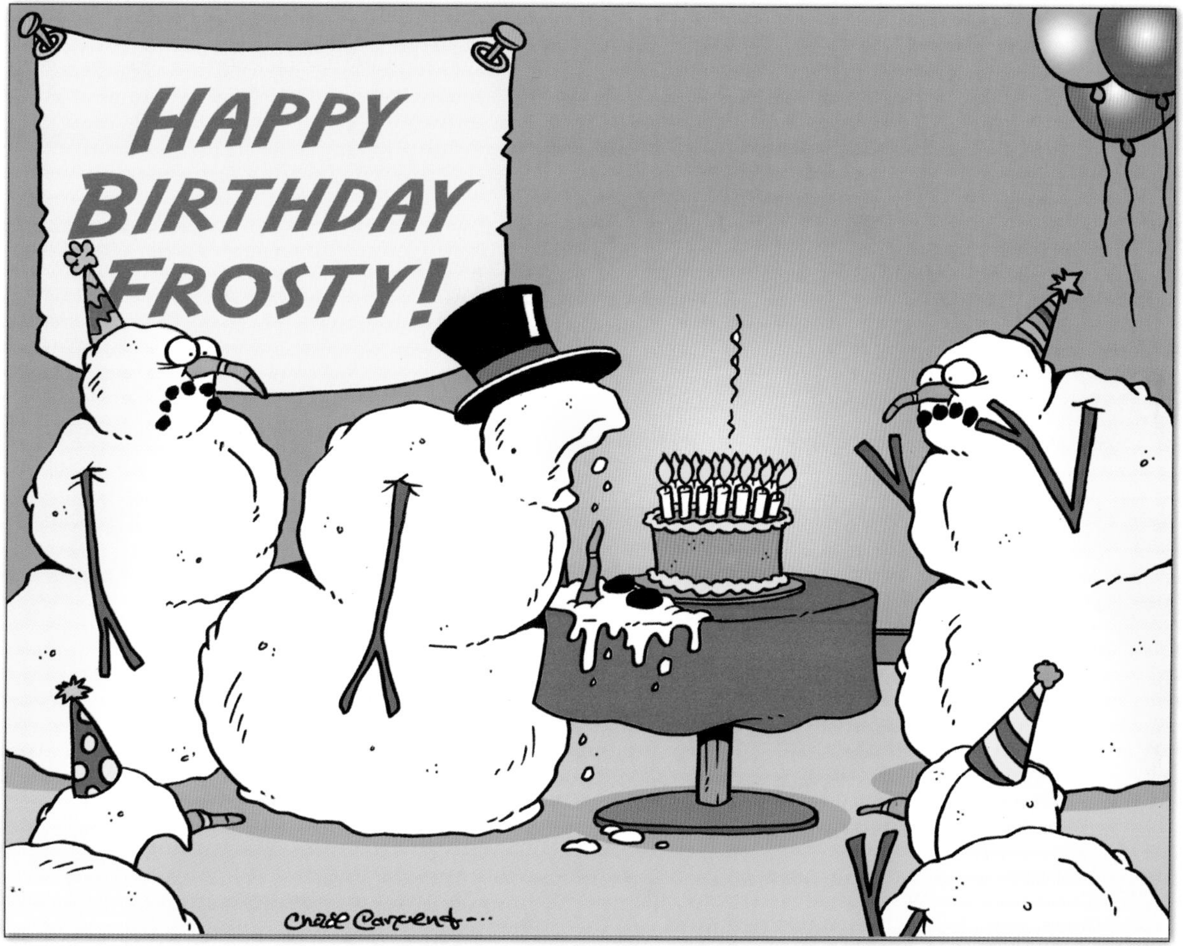
HAPPY
BIRTHDAY
FROSTY!

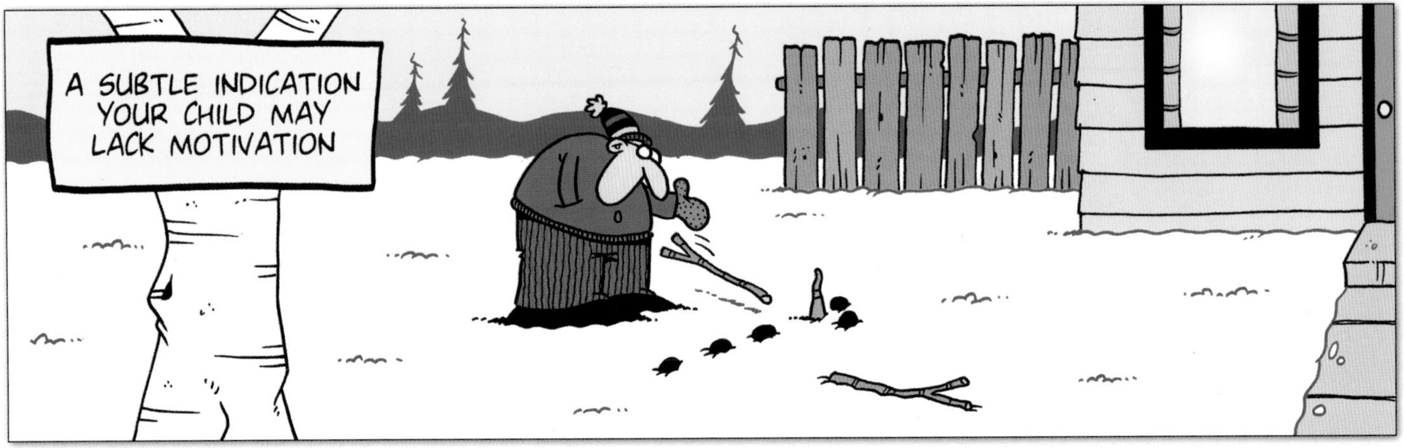
A SUBTLE INDICATION YOUR CHILD MAY LACK MOTIVATION

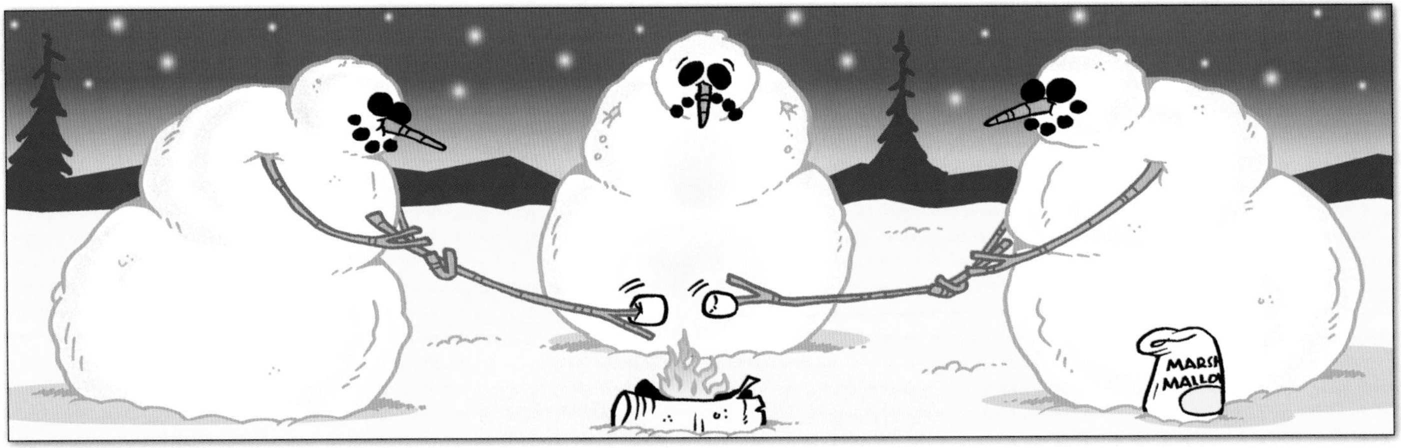
MARSH
MALLO

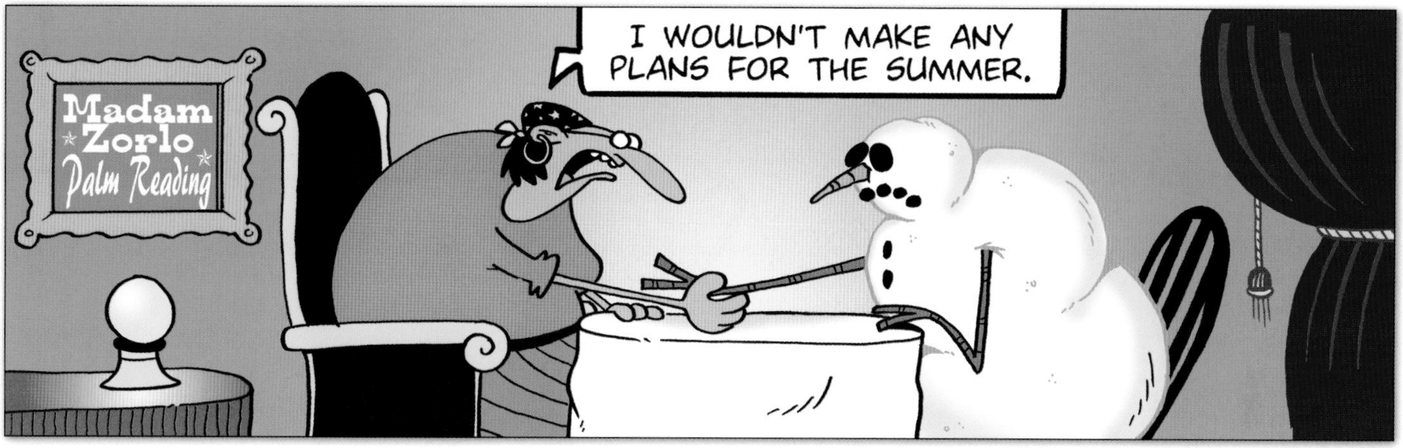
Madam
Zorlo
Palm Reading
I WOULDN'T MAKE ANY PLANS FOR THE SUMMER.

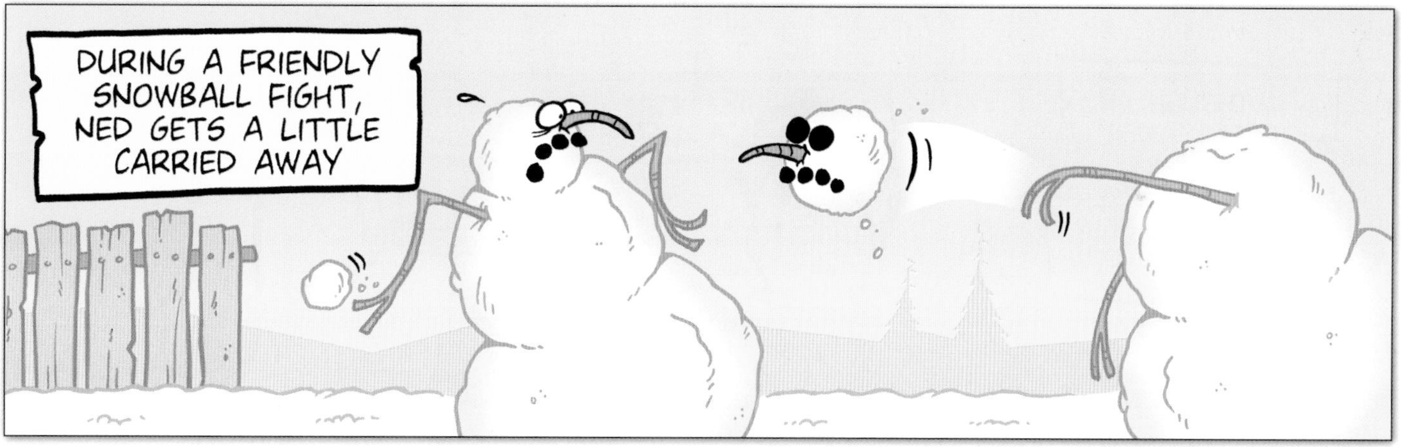
DURING A FRIENDLY SNOWBALL FIGHT, NED GETS A LITTLE CARRIED AWAY

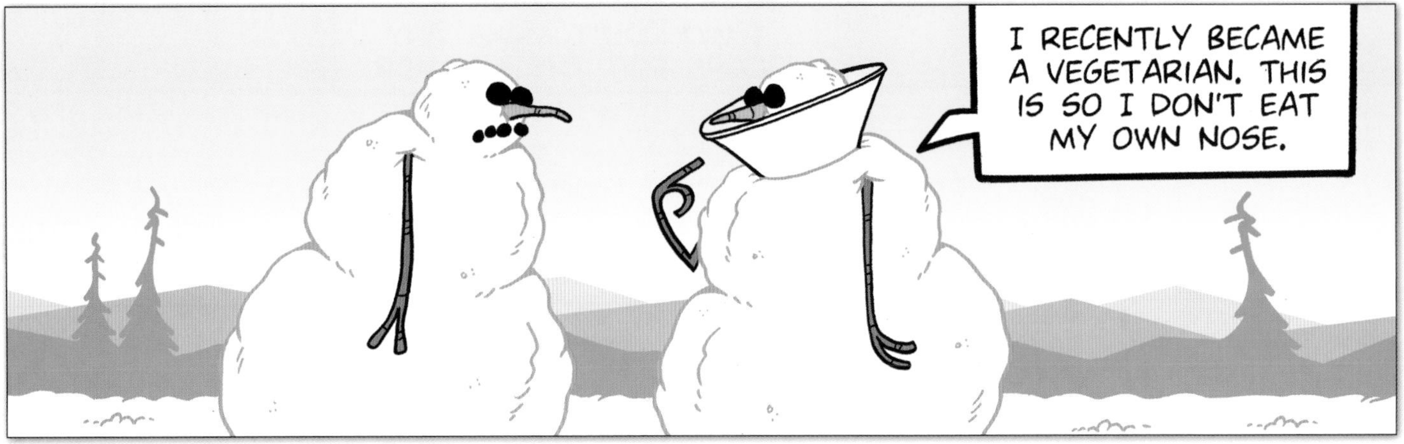
I RECENTLY BECAME A VEGETARIAN. THIS IS SO I DON'T EAT MY OWN NOSE.

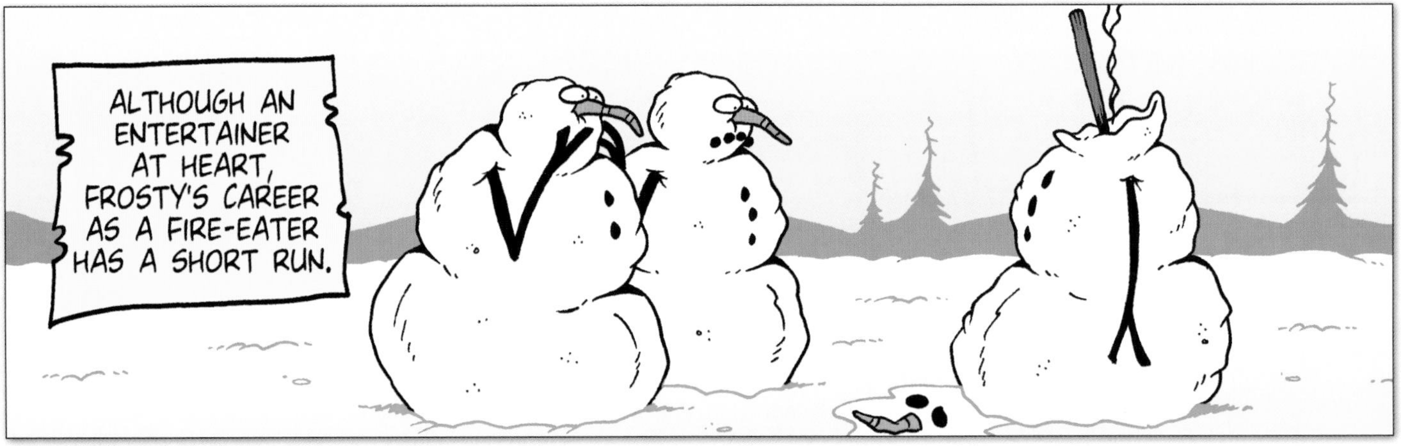
ALTHOUGH AN ENTERTAINER AT HEART, FROSTY'S CAREER AS A FIRE-EATER HAS A SHORT RUN.

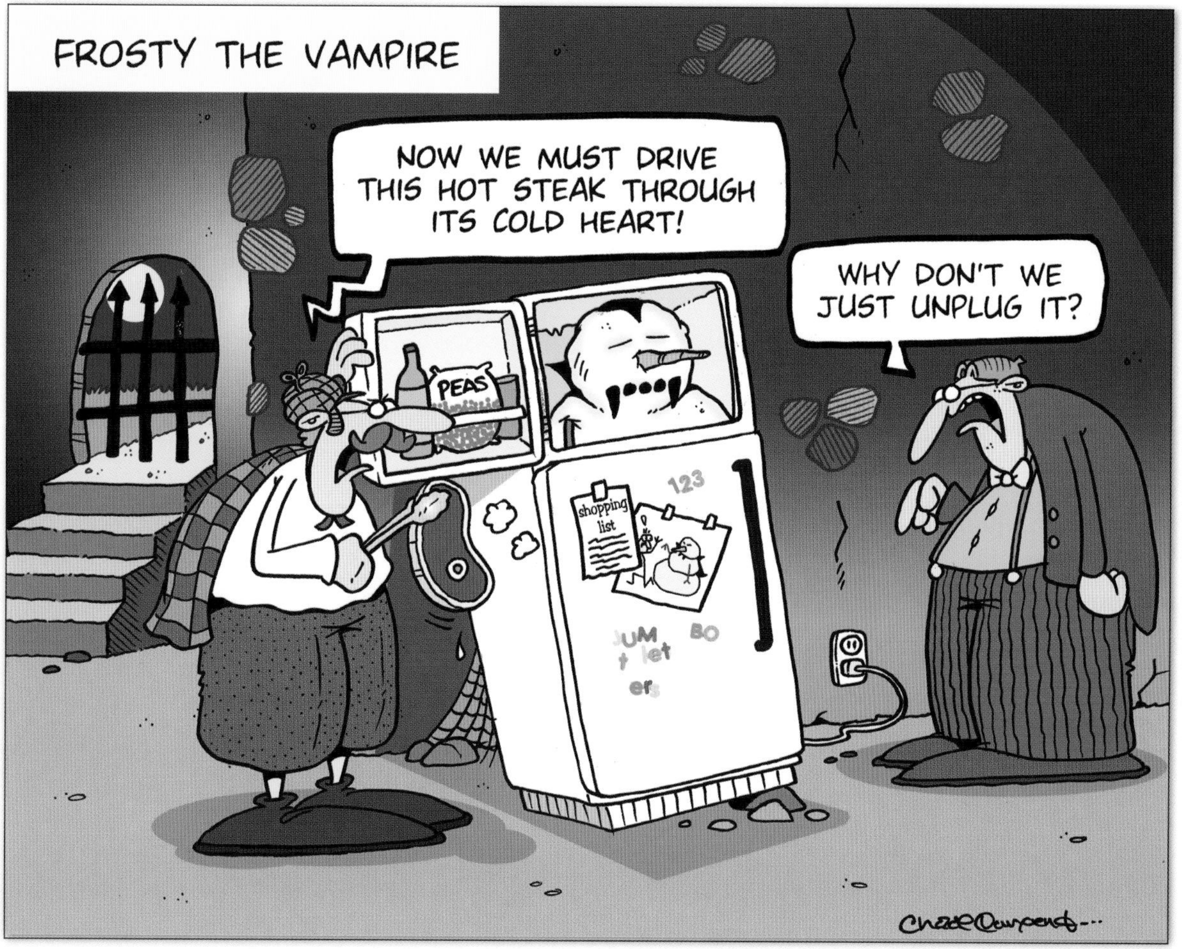
FROSTY THE VAMPIRE
NOW WE MUST DRIVE THIS HOT STEAK THROUGH ITS COLD HEART!
WHY DON'T WE JUST UNPLUG IT?
PEAS
shopping list
123

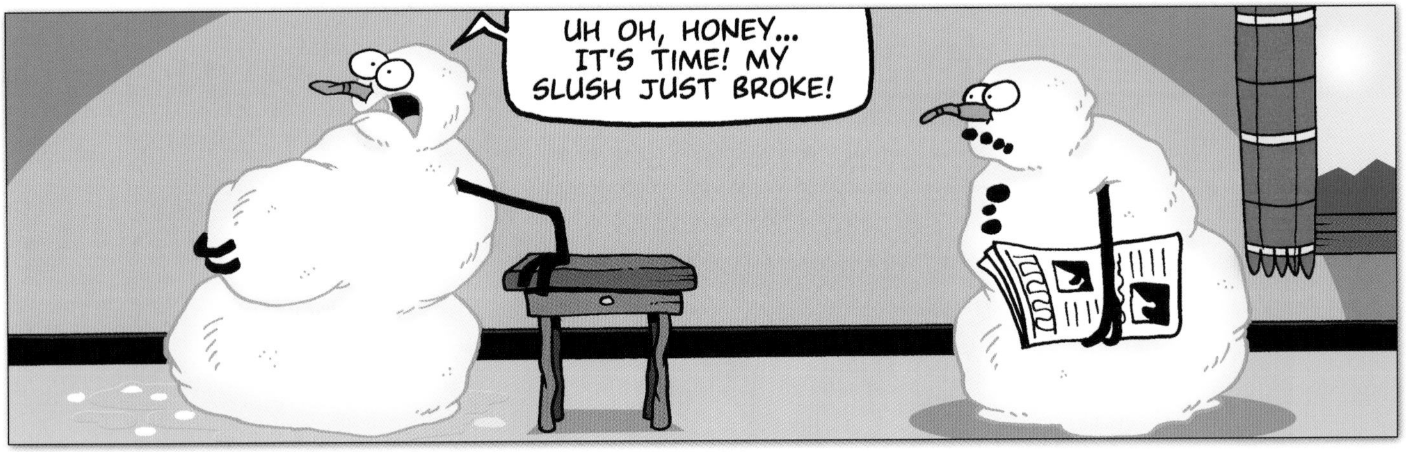
UH OH, HONEY... IT'S TIME! MY SLUSH JUST BROKE!

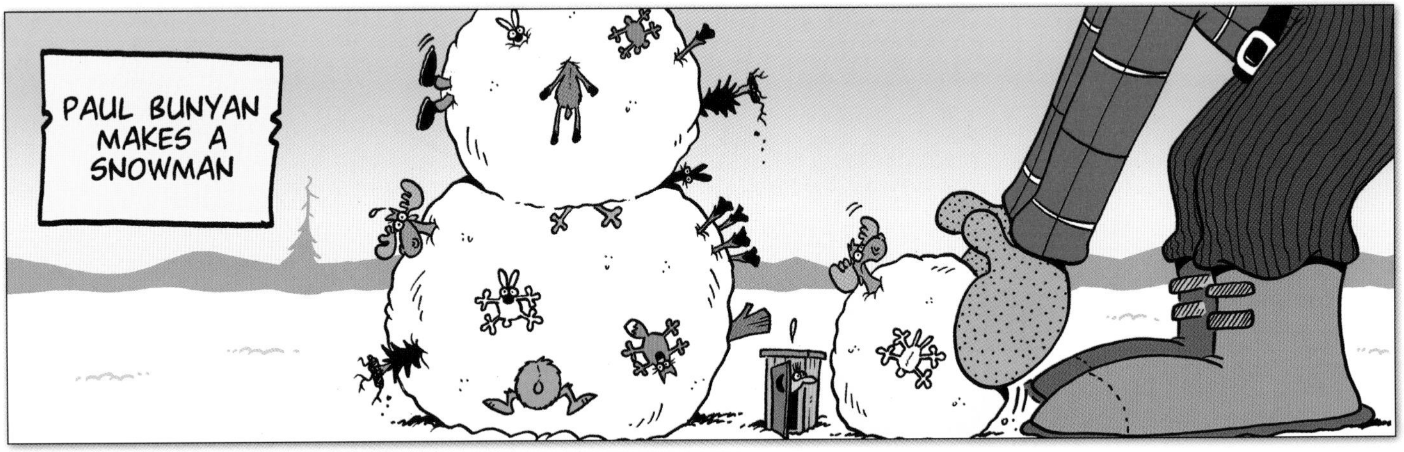
PAUL BUNYAN MAKES A SNOWMAN

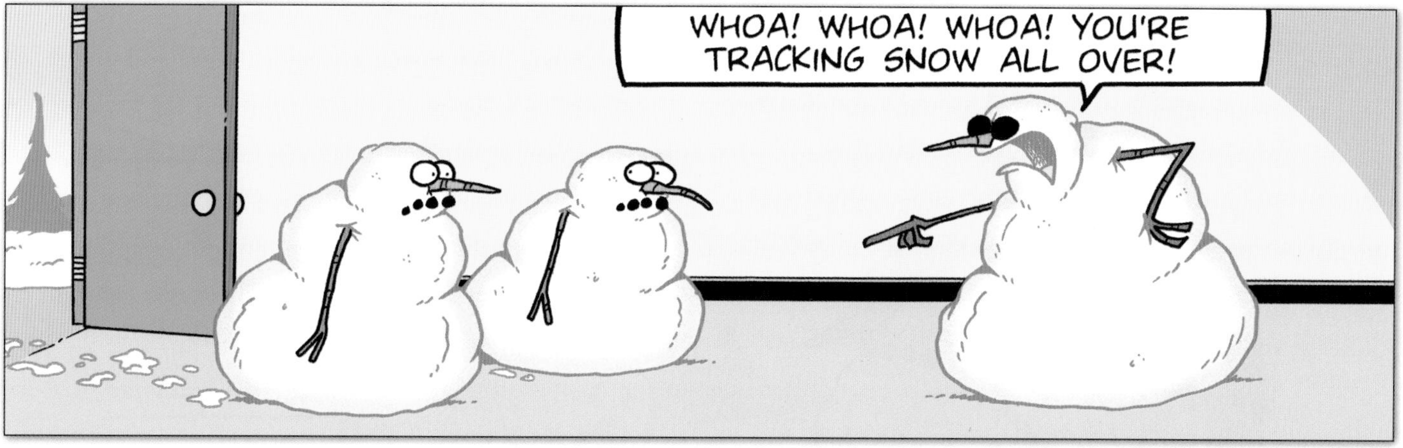
WHOA! WHOA! WHOA! YOU'RE TRACKING SNOW ALL OVER!

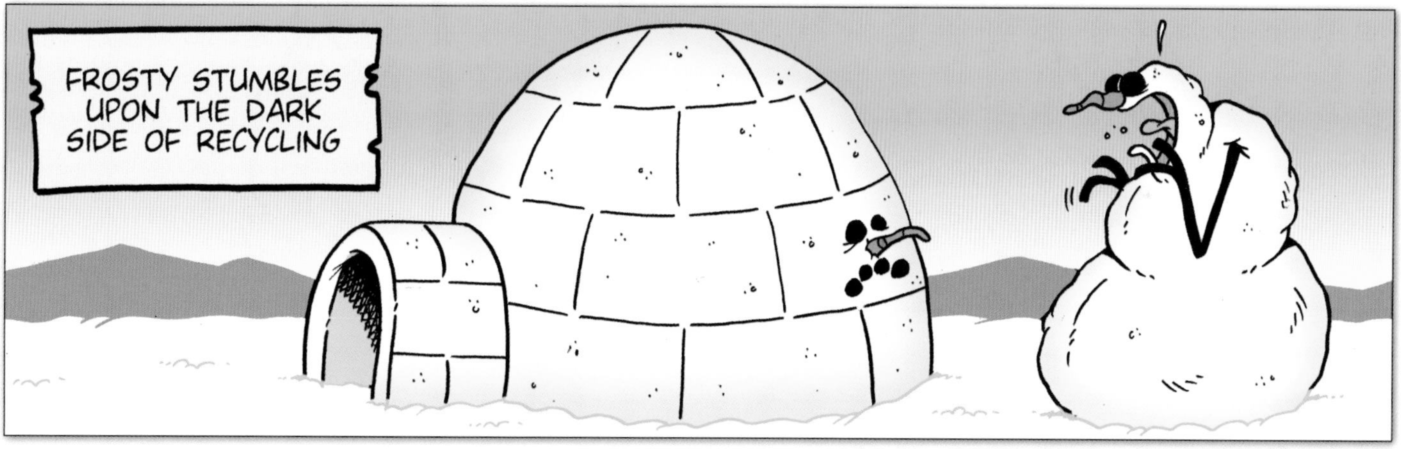
FROSTY STUMBLES UPON THE DARK SIDE OF RECYCLING

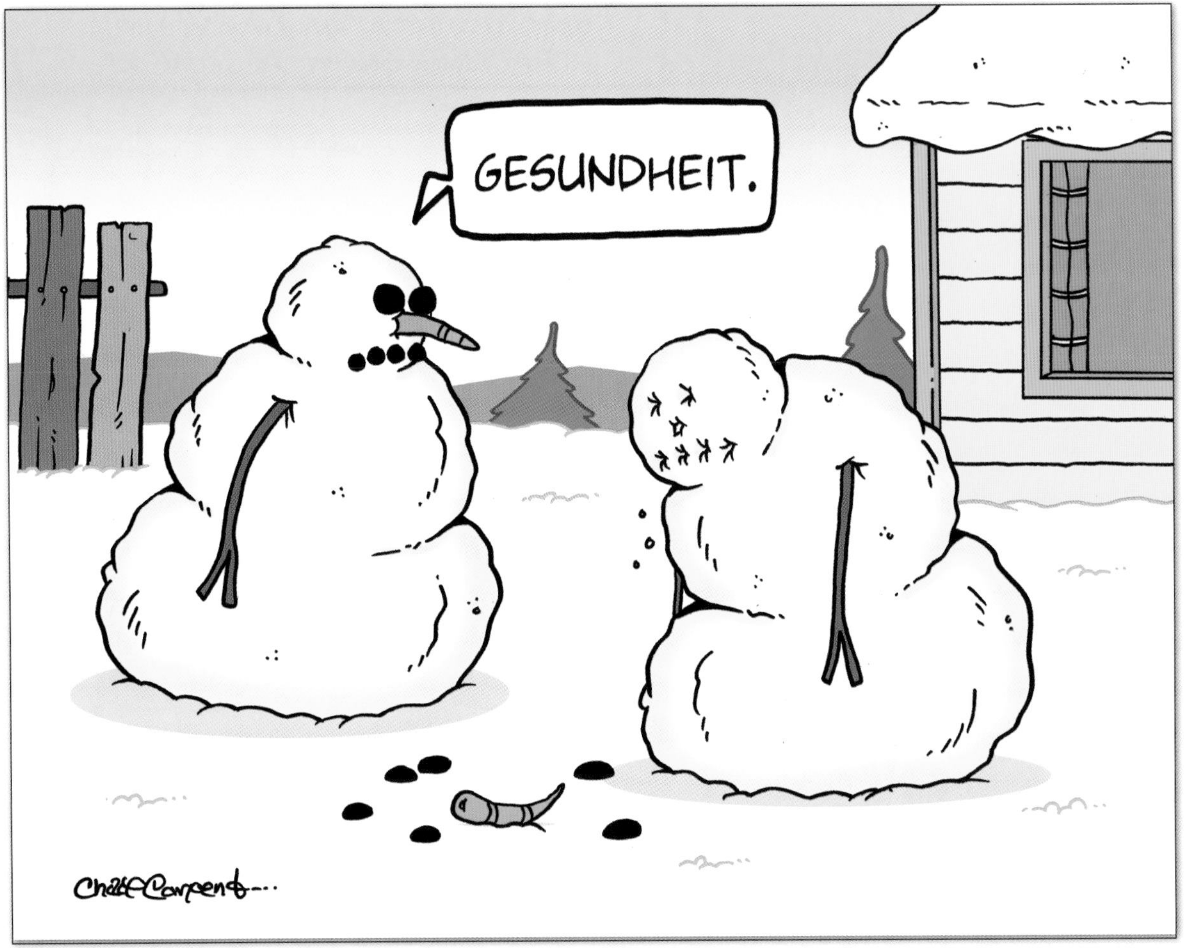
GESUNDHEIT.
ChadCarpenter

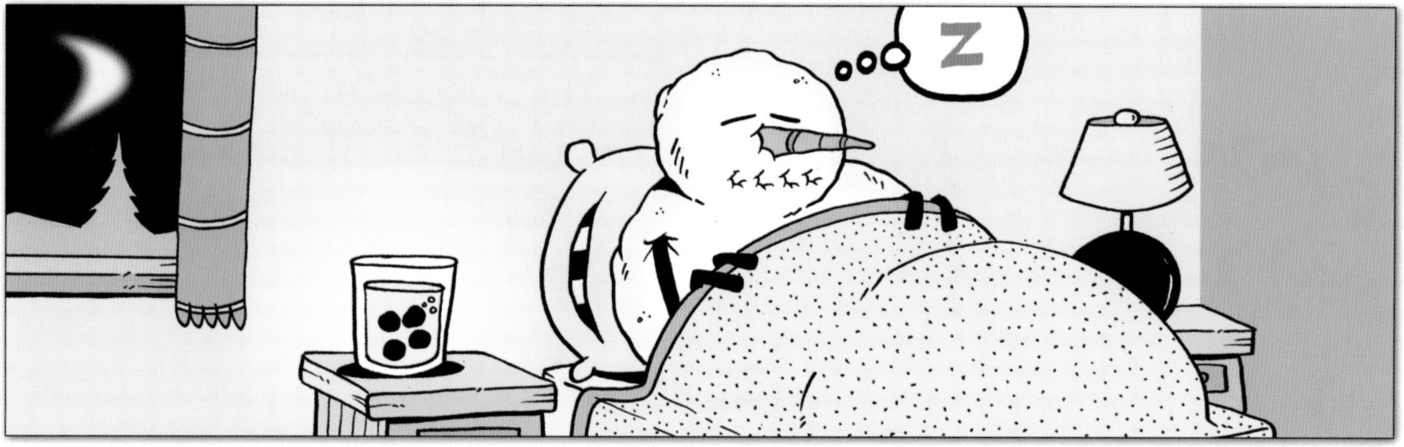
Z

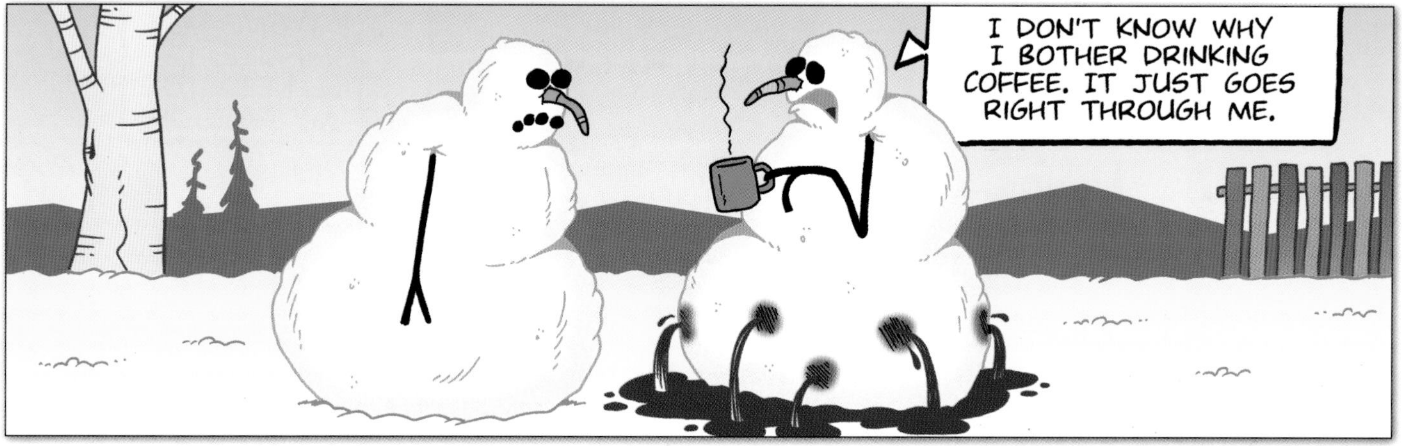
I DON'T KNOW WHY I BOTHER DRINKING COFFEE. IT JUST GOES RIGHT THROUGH ME.

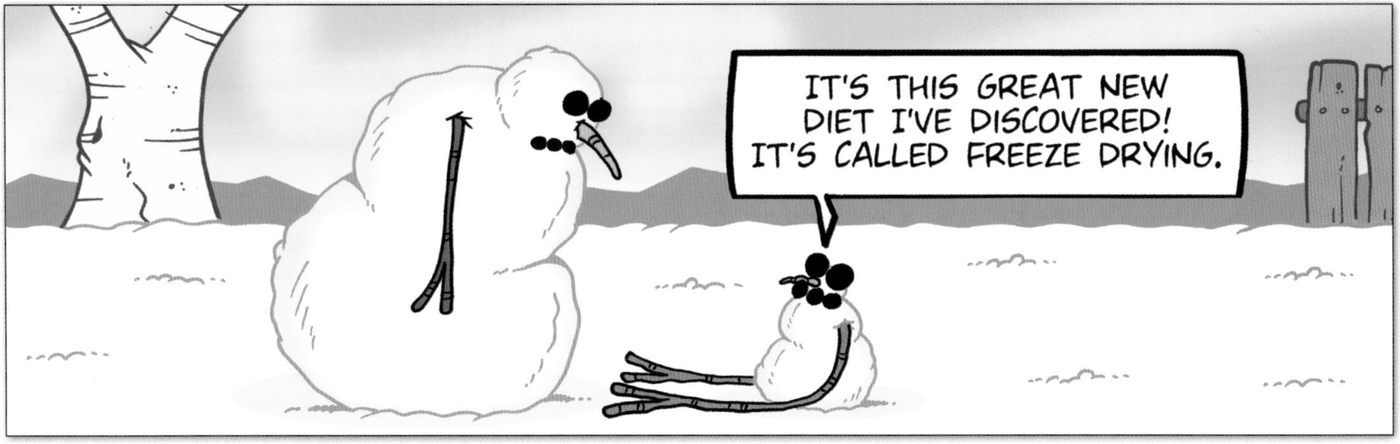
IT'S THIS GREAT NEW DIET I'VE DISCOVERED! IT'S CALLED FREEZE DRYING.

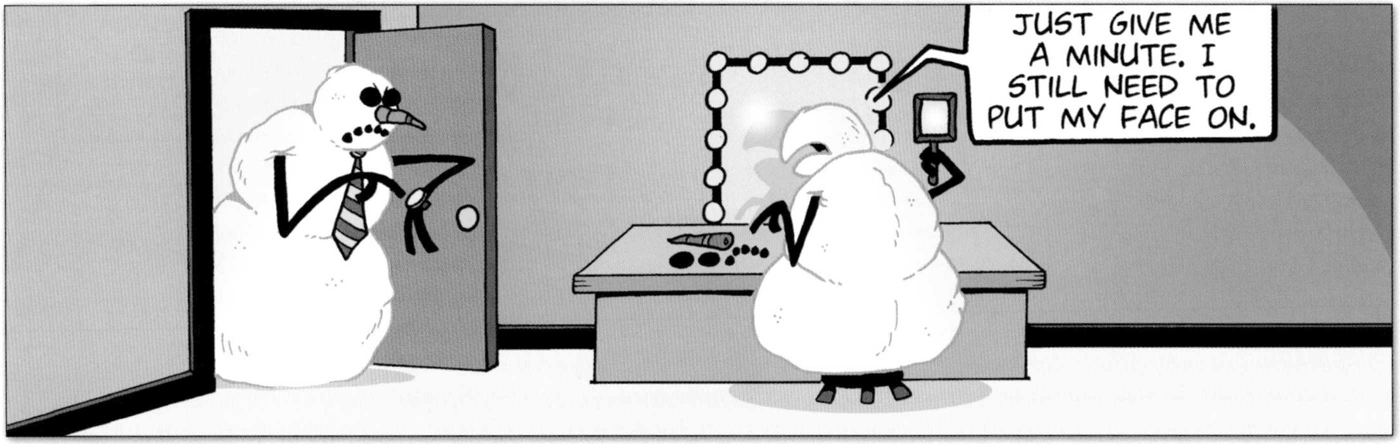
JUST GIVE ME A MINUTE. I STILL NEED TO PUT MY FACE ON.

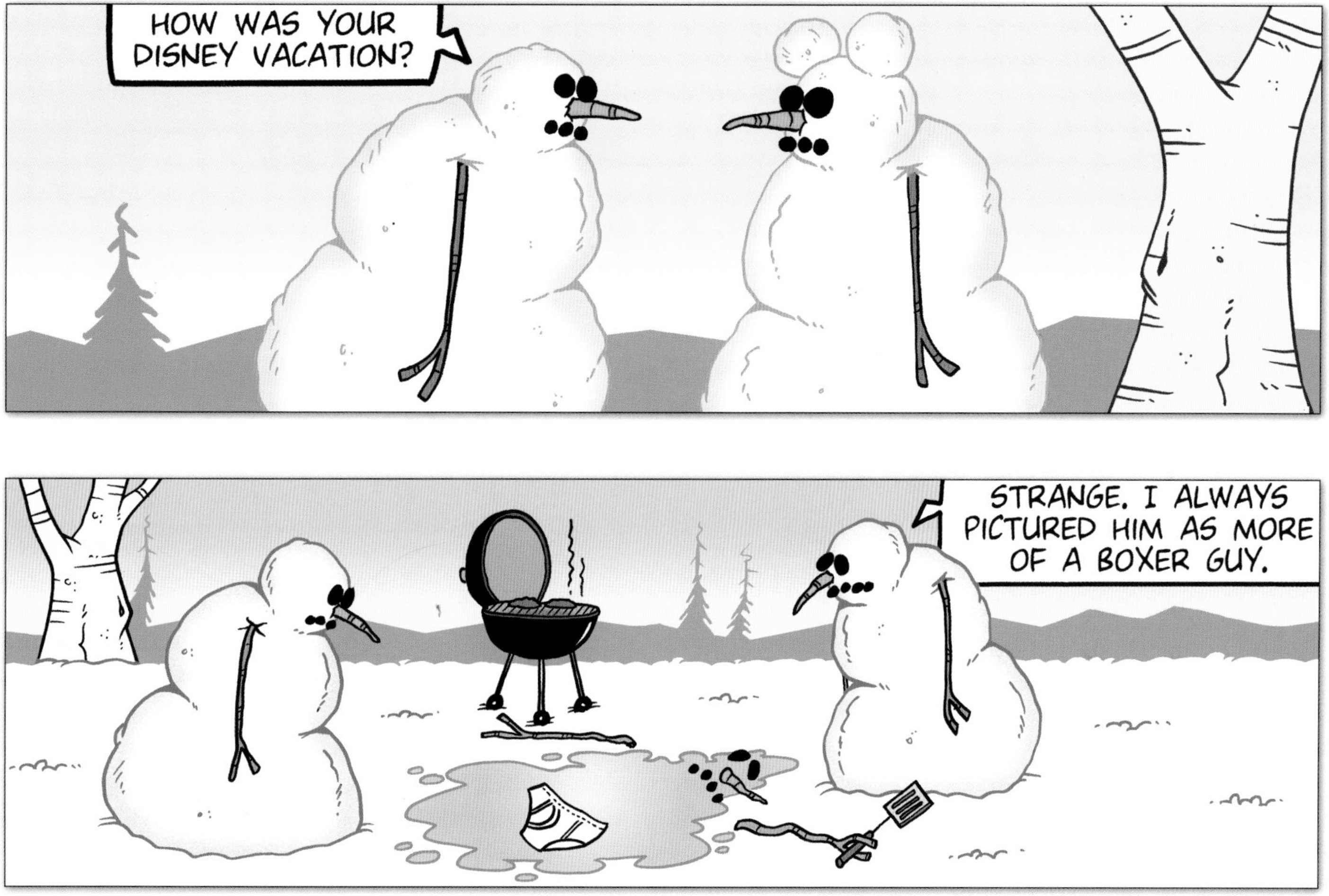
HOW WAS YOUR DISNEY VACATION?
STRANGE. I ALWAYS PICTURED HIM AS MORE OF A BOXER GUY.

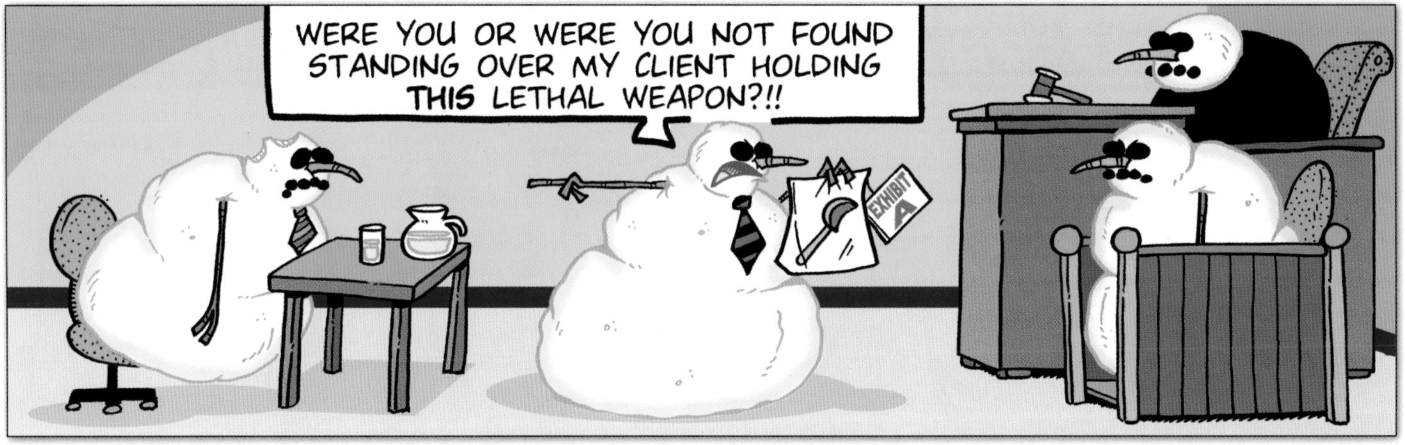
WERE YOU OR WERE YOU NOT FOUND STANDING OVER MY CLIENT HOLDING **THIS** LETHAL WEAPON?!!
EXHIBIT A

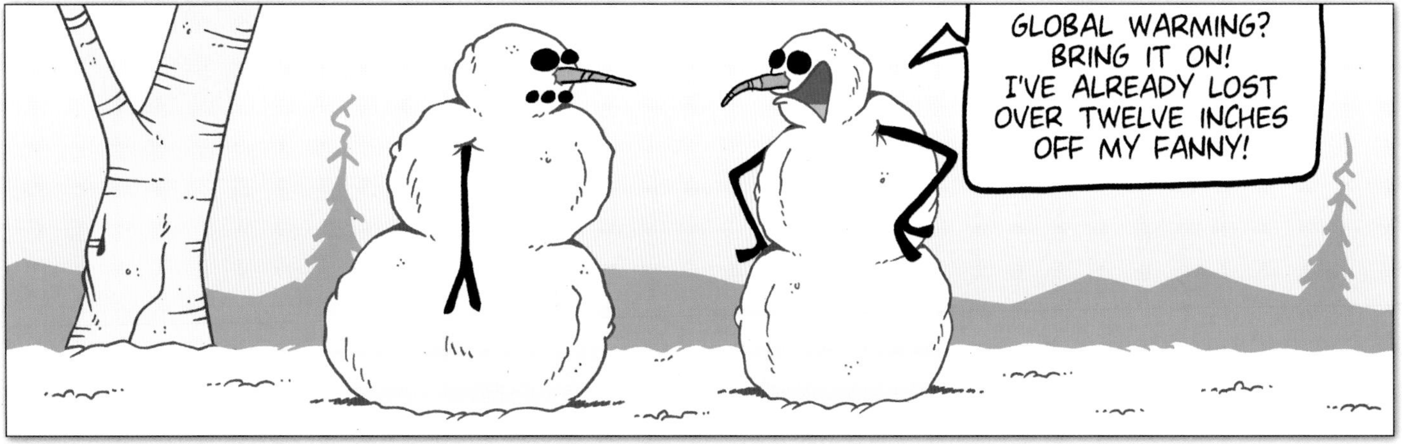
GLOBAL WARMING? BRING IT ON! I'VE ALREADY LOST OVER TWELVE INCHES OFF MY FANNY!

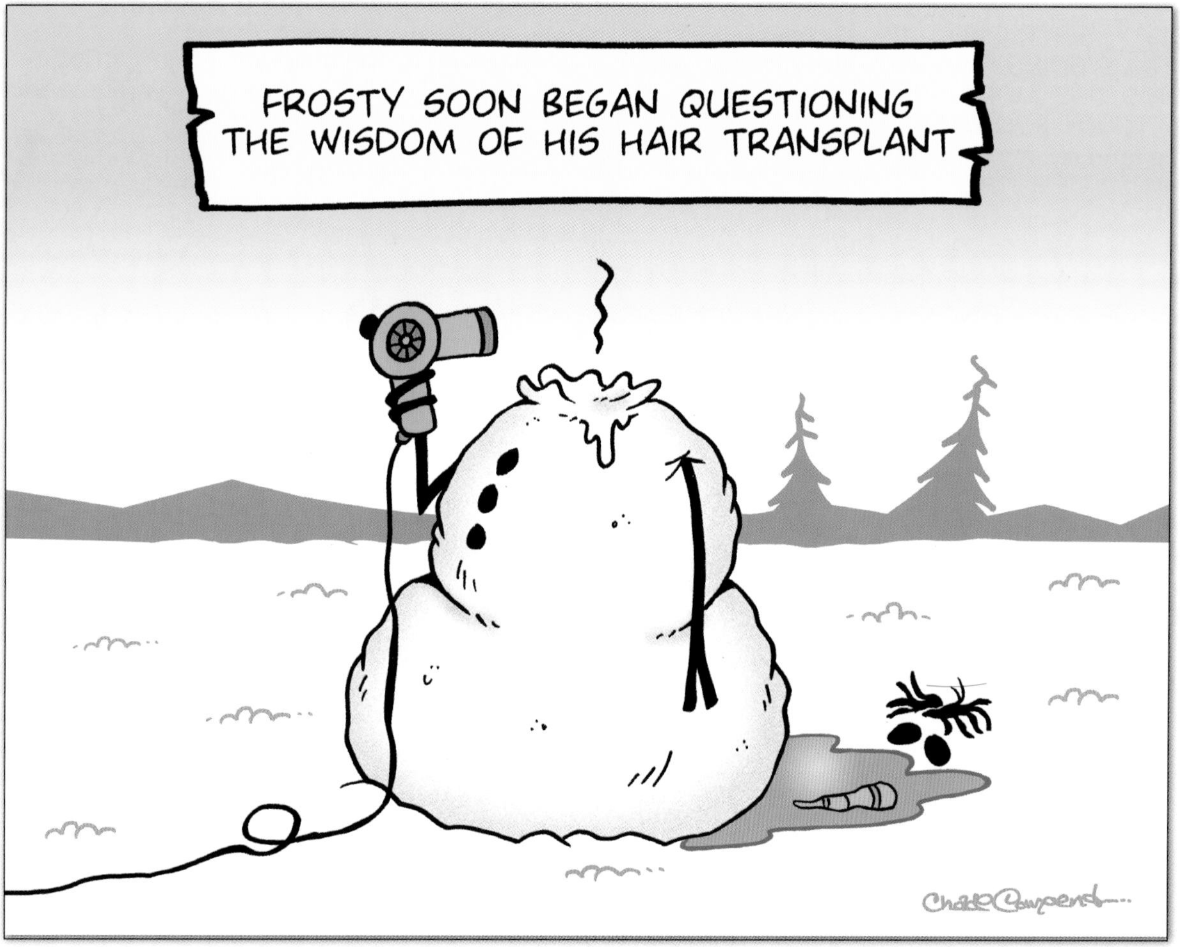
FROSTY SOON BEGAN QUESTIONING
THE WISDOM OF HIS HAIR TRANSPLANT

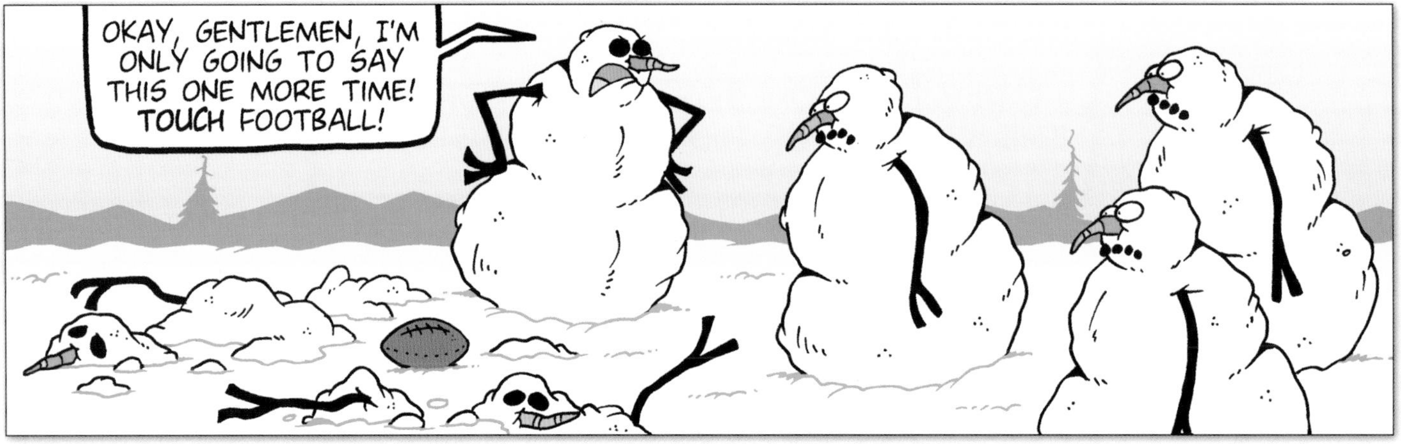
OKAY, GENTLEMEN, I'M ONLY GOING TO SAY THIS ONE MORE TIME! TOUCH FOOTBALL!

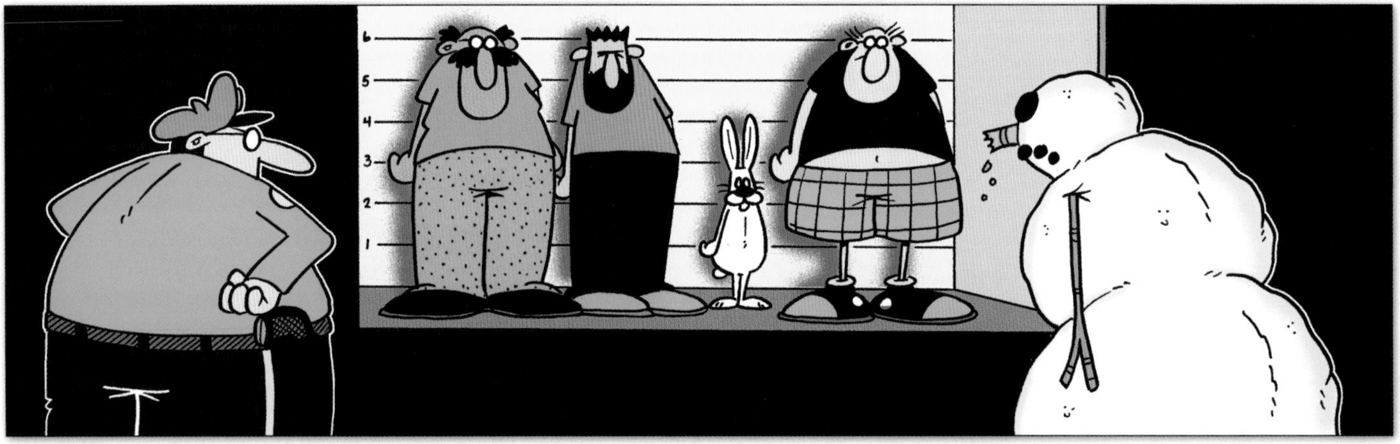

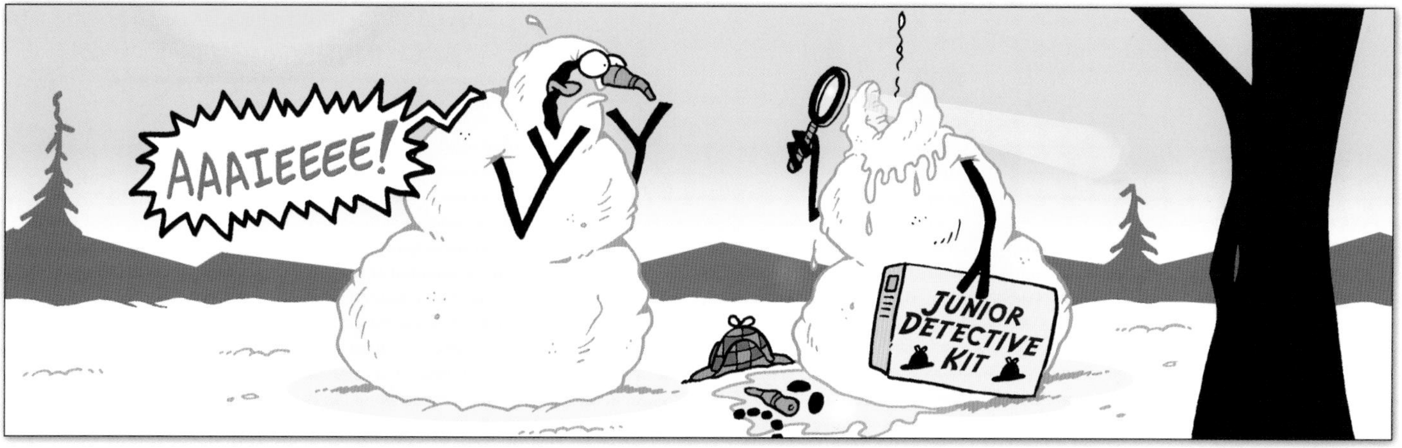
AAAIEEEE!
JUNIOR DETECTIVE KIT

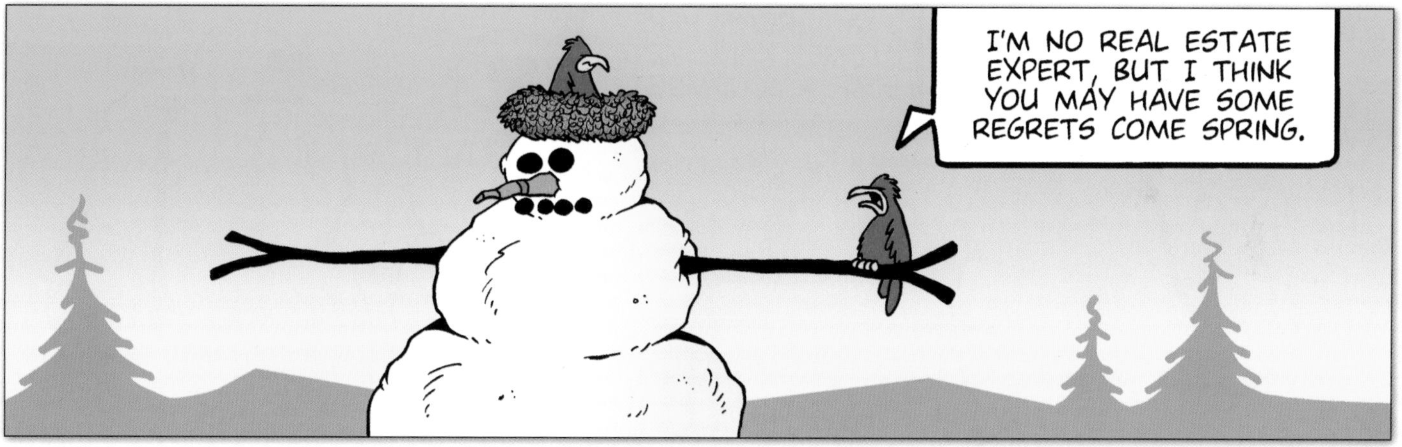
I'M NO REAL ESTATE EXPERT, BUT I THINK YOU MAY HAVE SOME REGRETS COME SPRING.

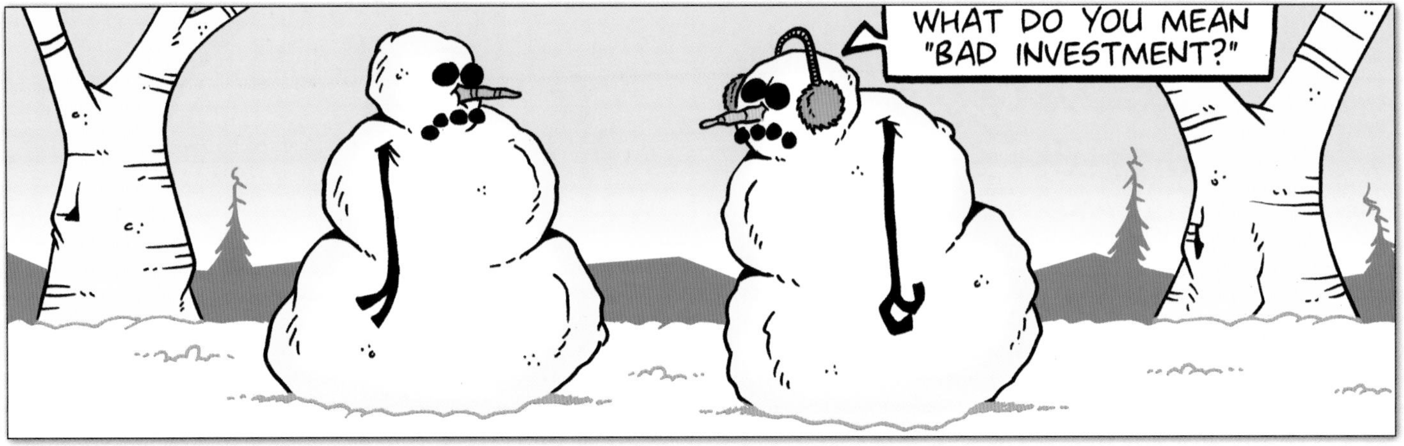
WHAT DO YOU MEAN "BAD INVESTMENT?"

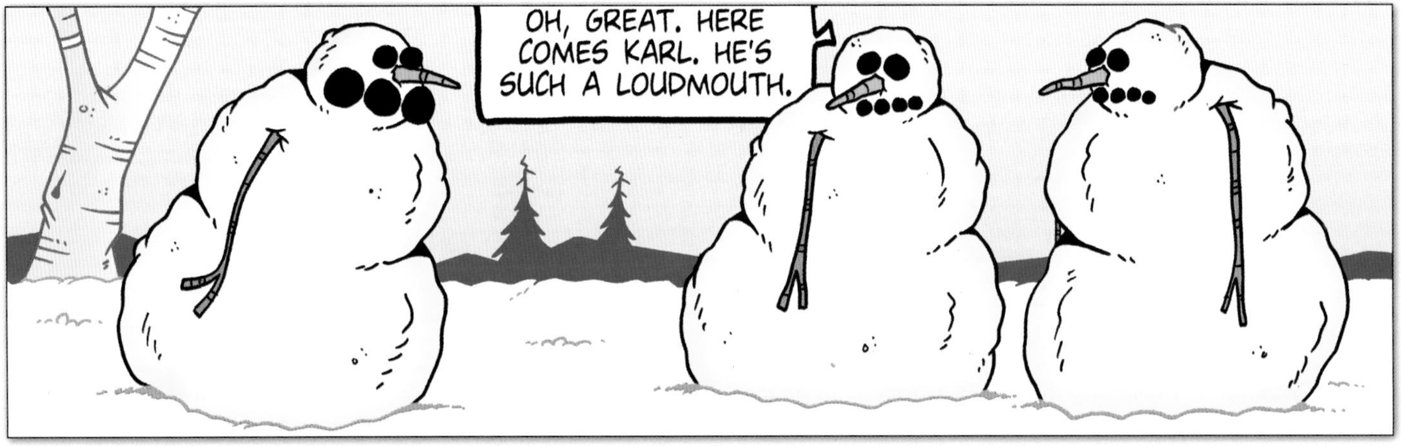
OH, GREAT. HERE COMES KARL. HE'S SUCH A LOUDMOUTH.

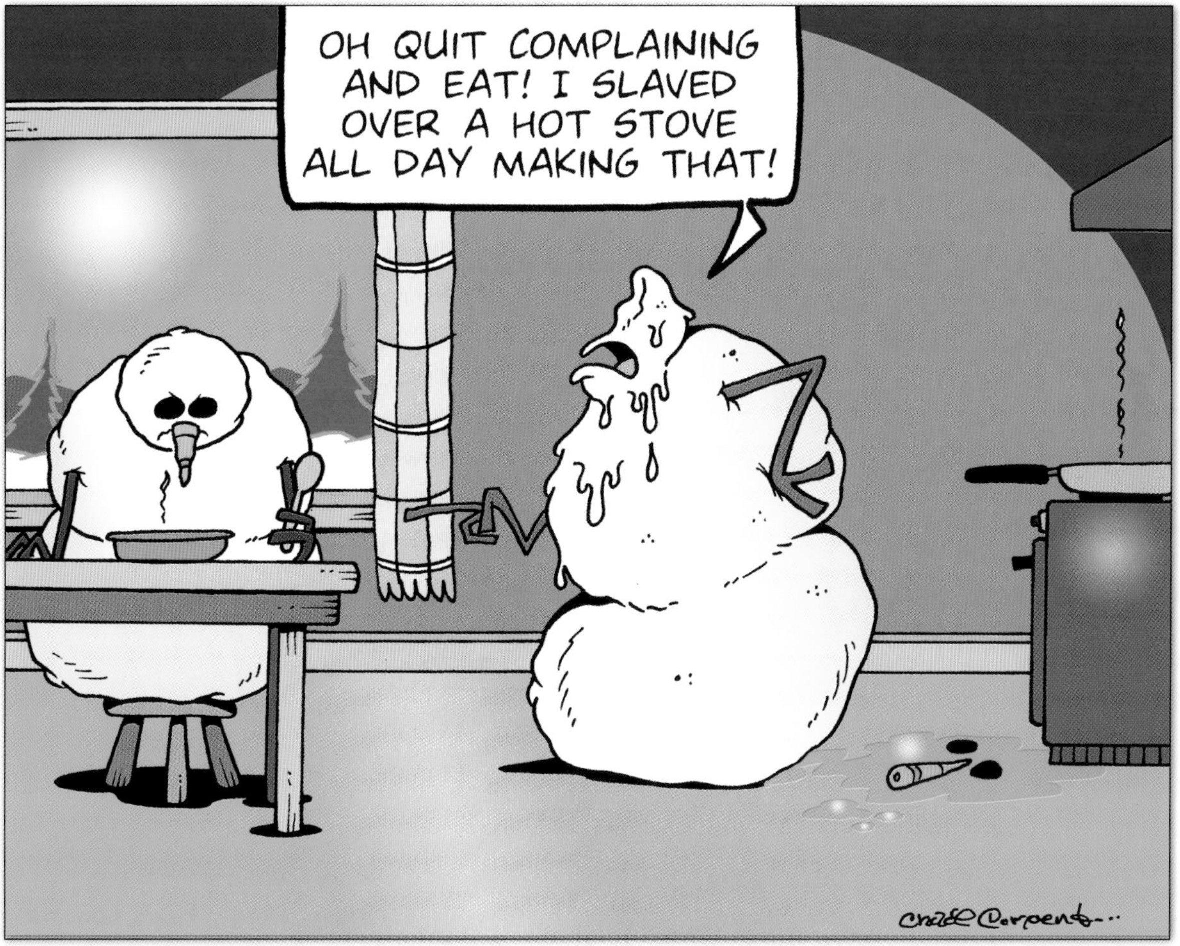
OH QUIT COMPLAINING AND EAT! I SLAVED OVER A HOT STOVE ALL DAY MAKING THAT!

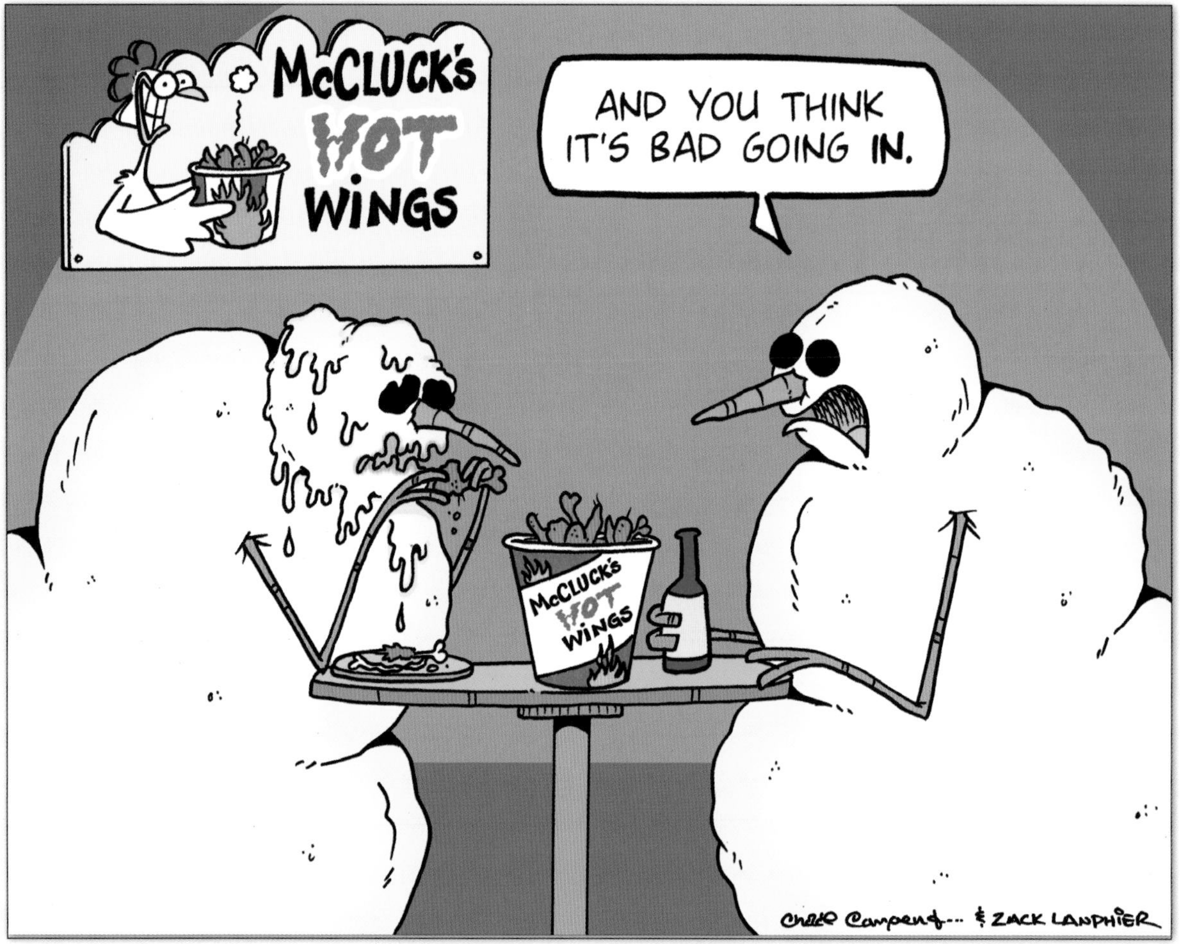
McCLUCK'S
HOT
WINGS
AND YOU THINK IT'S BAD GOING IN.
McCLUCK'S
HOT
WINGS

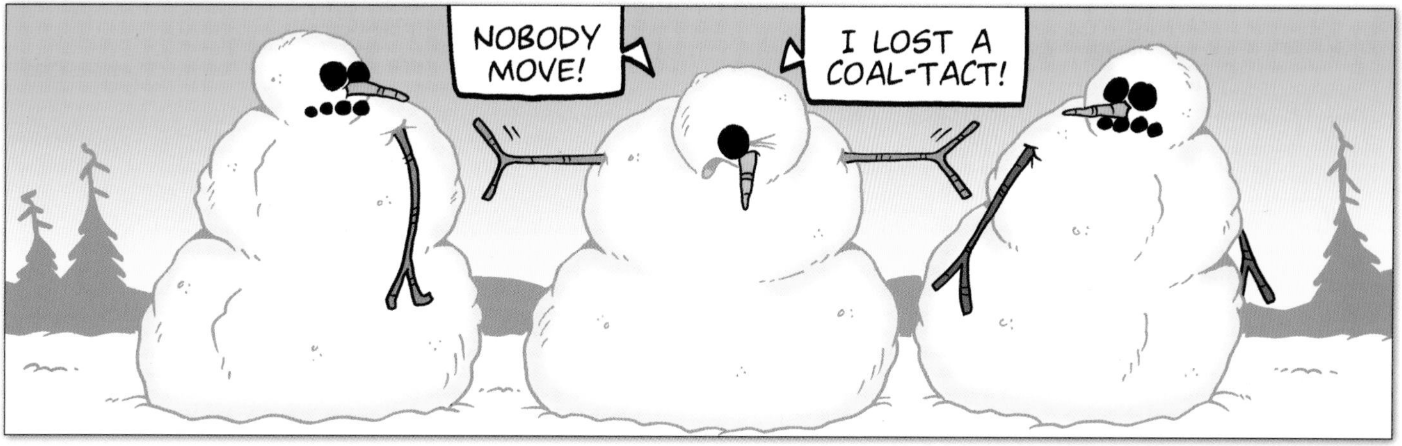
NOBODY MOVE!
I LOST A COAL-TACT!

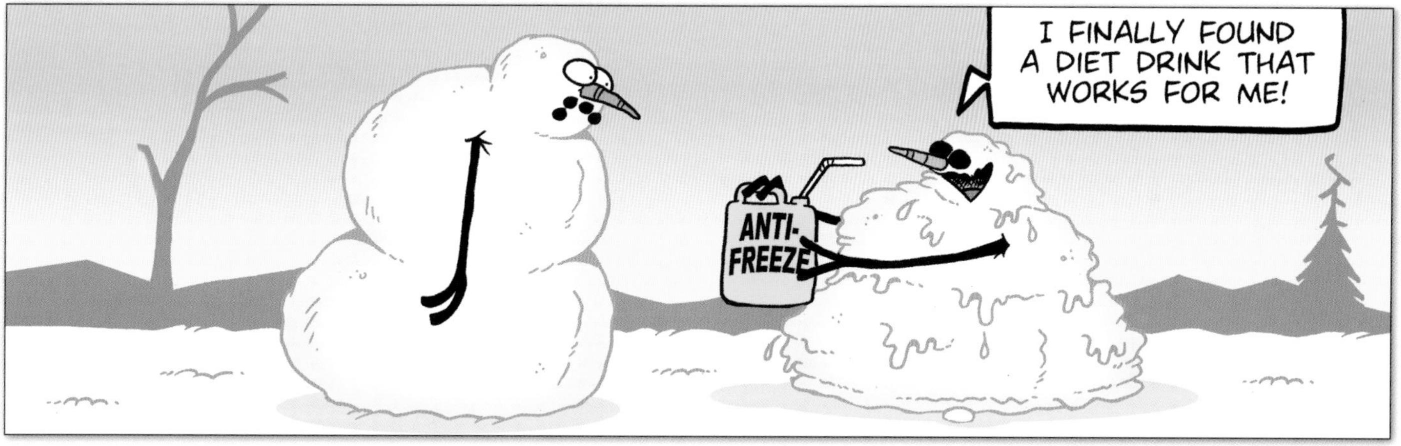
I FINALLY FOUND A DIET DRINK THAT WORKS FOR ME!
ANTI-FREEZE

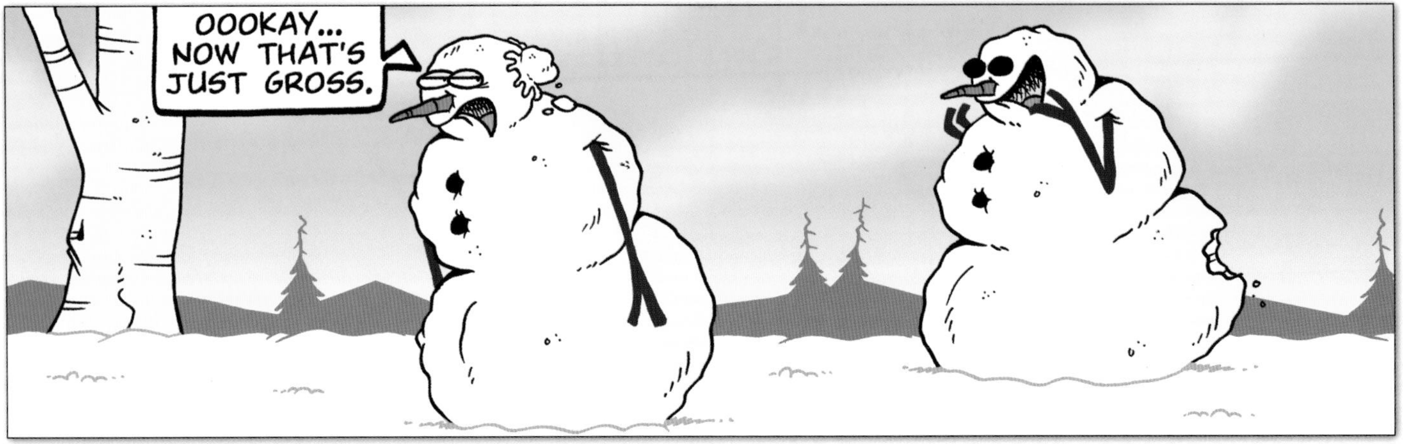
OOOKAY... NOW THAT'S JUST GROSS.

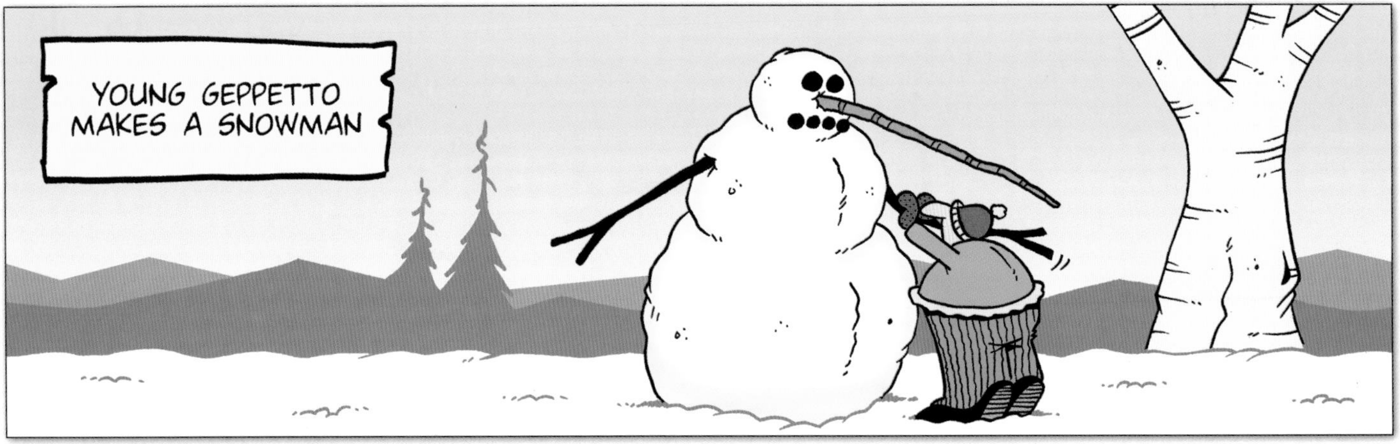
YOUNG GEPPETTO MAKES A SNOWMAN

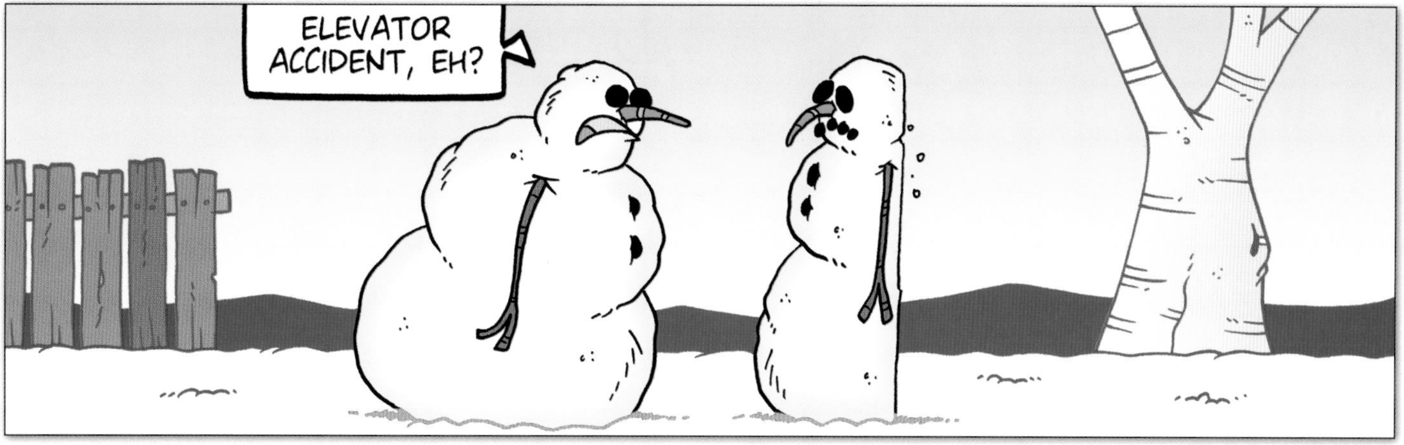
ELEVATOR ACCIDENT, EH?

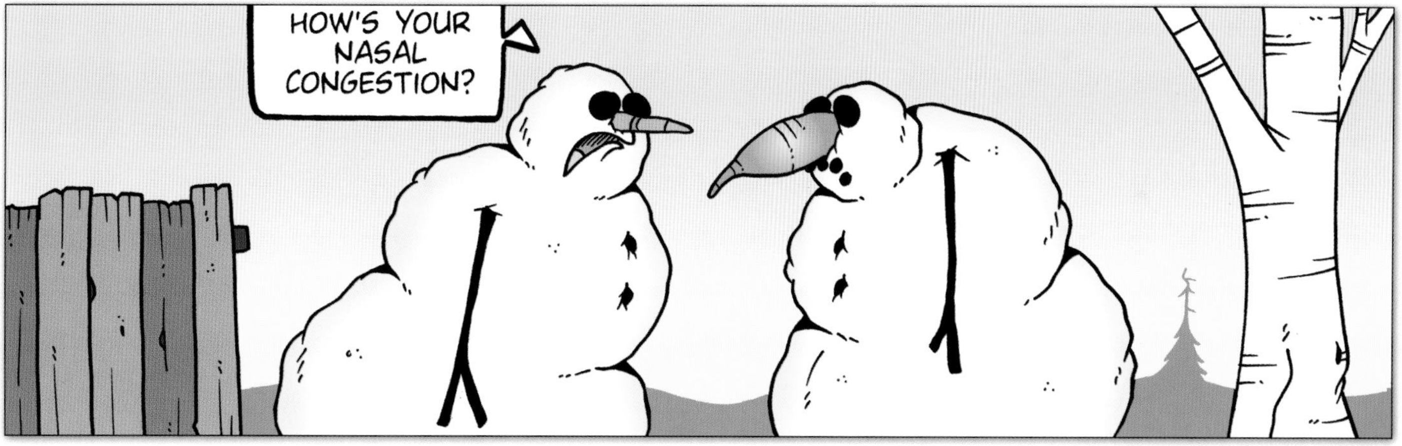
HOW'S YOUR NASAL CONGESTION?

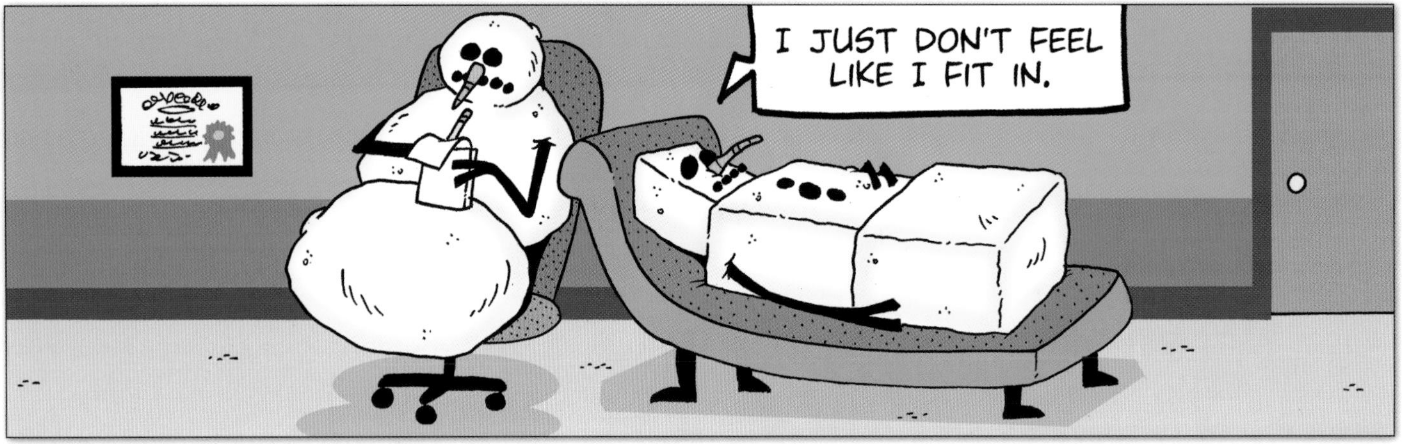
I JUST DON'T FEEL LIKE I FIT IN.

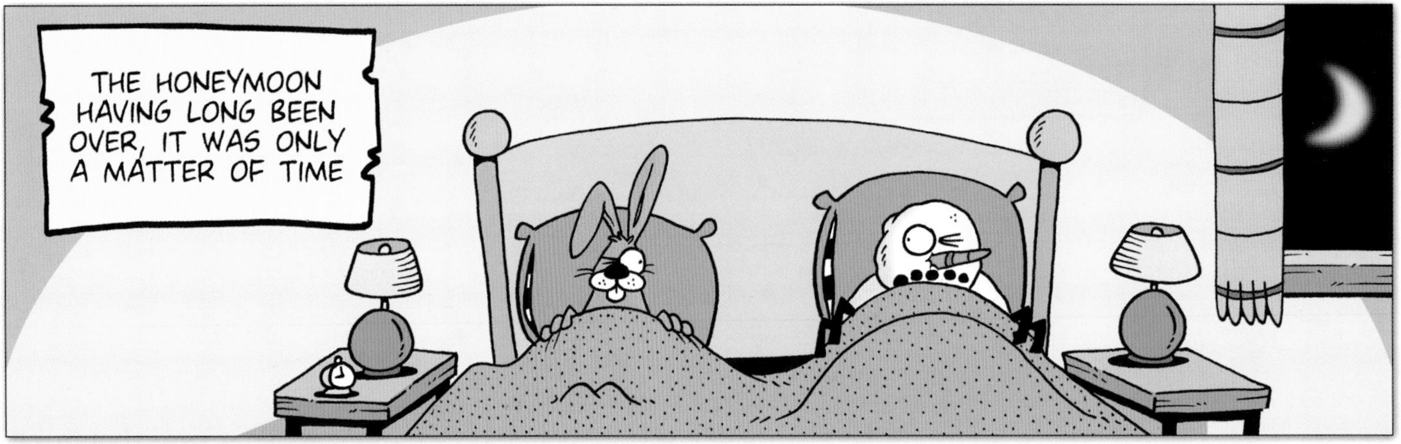
THE HONEYMOON HAVING LONG BEEN OVER, IT WAS ONLY A MATTER OF TIME

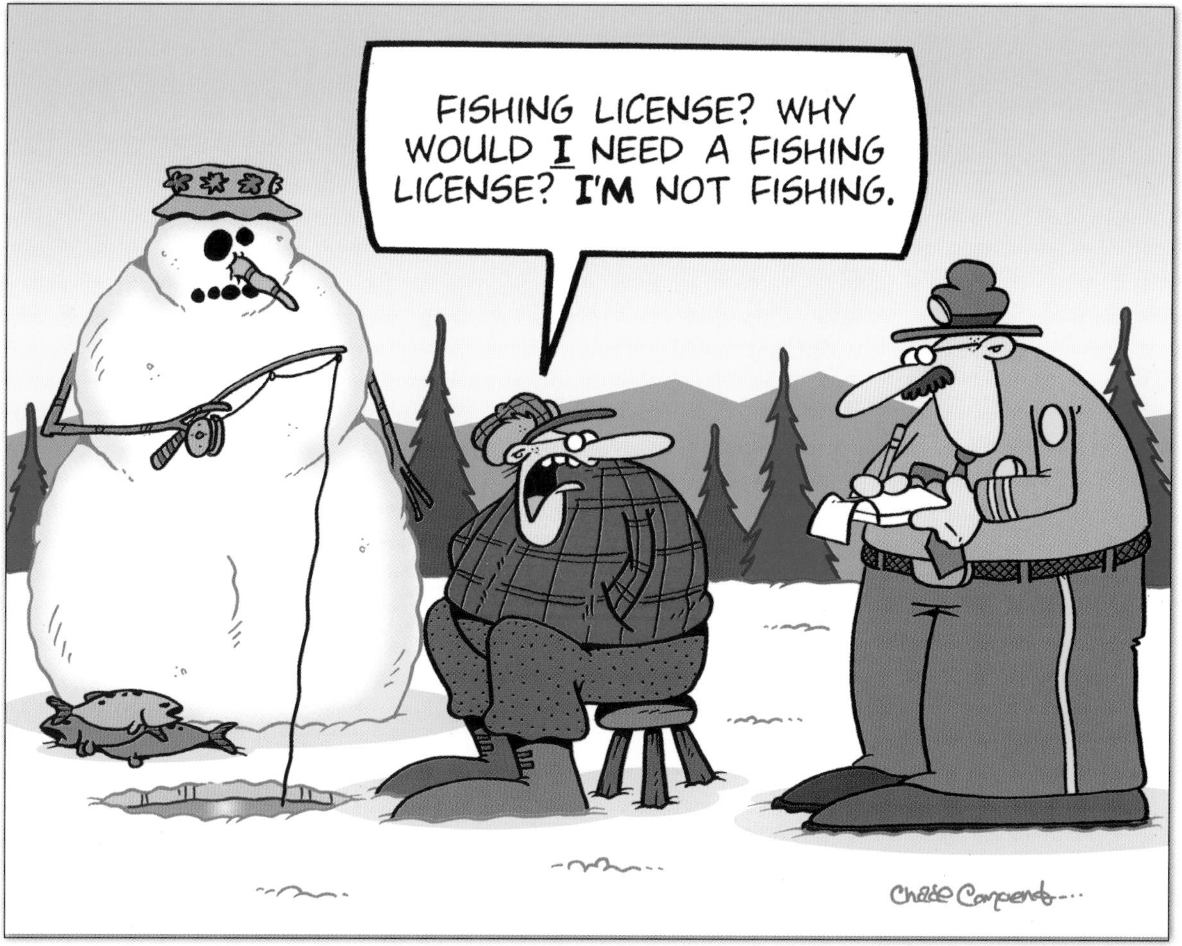
FISHING LICENSE? WHY WOULD I NEED A FISHING LICENSE? I'M NOT FISHING.
Chad Carpenter

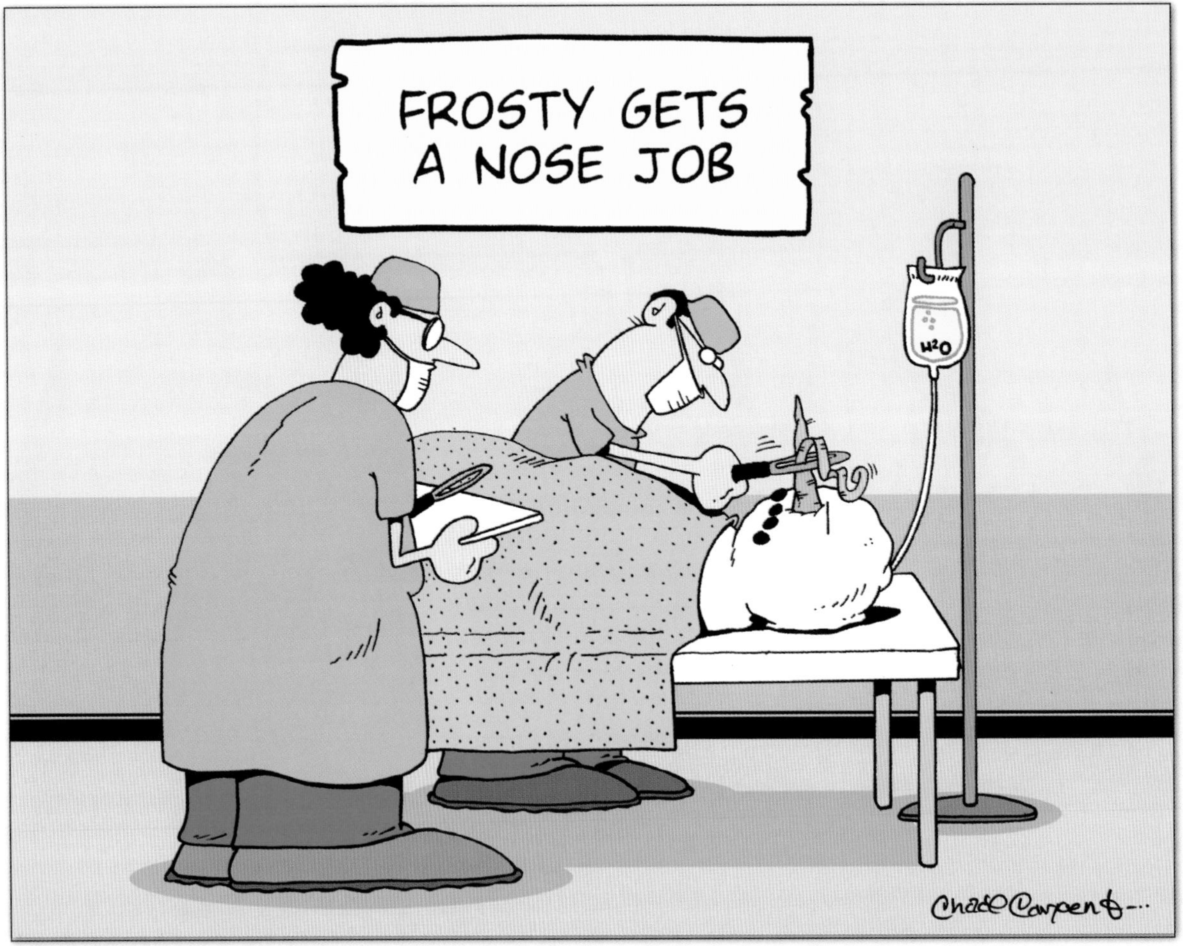
FROSTY GETS A NOSE JOB
H2O
Chad Carpenter

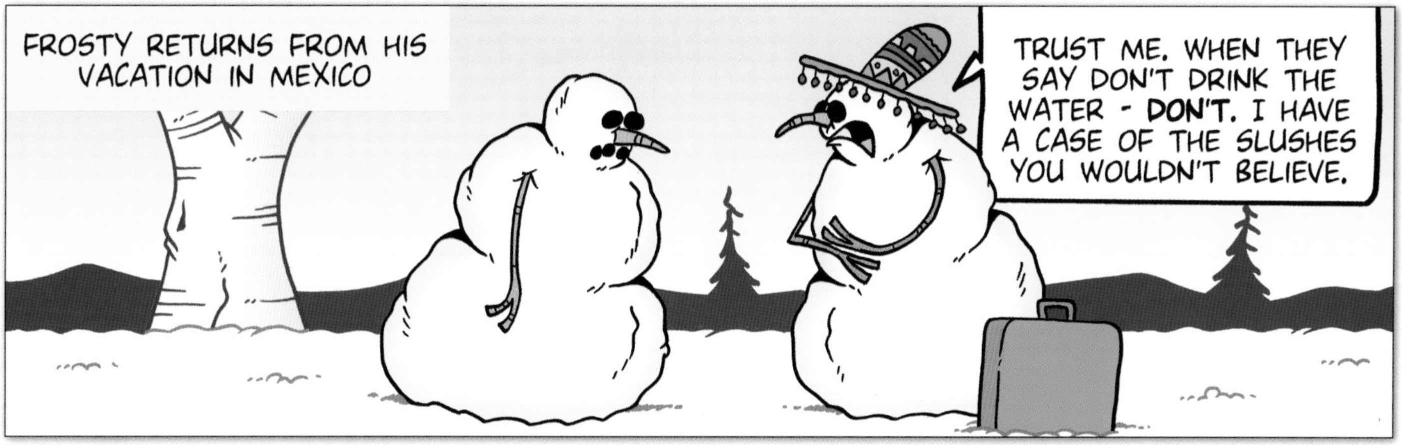
FROSTY RETURNS FROM HIS VACATION IN MEXICO
TRUST ME. WHEN THEY SAY DON'T DRINK THE WATER - **DON'T.** I HAVE A CASE OF THE SLUSHES YOU WOULDN'T BELIEVE.

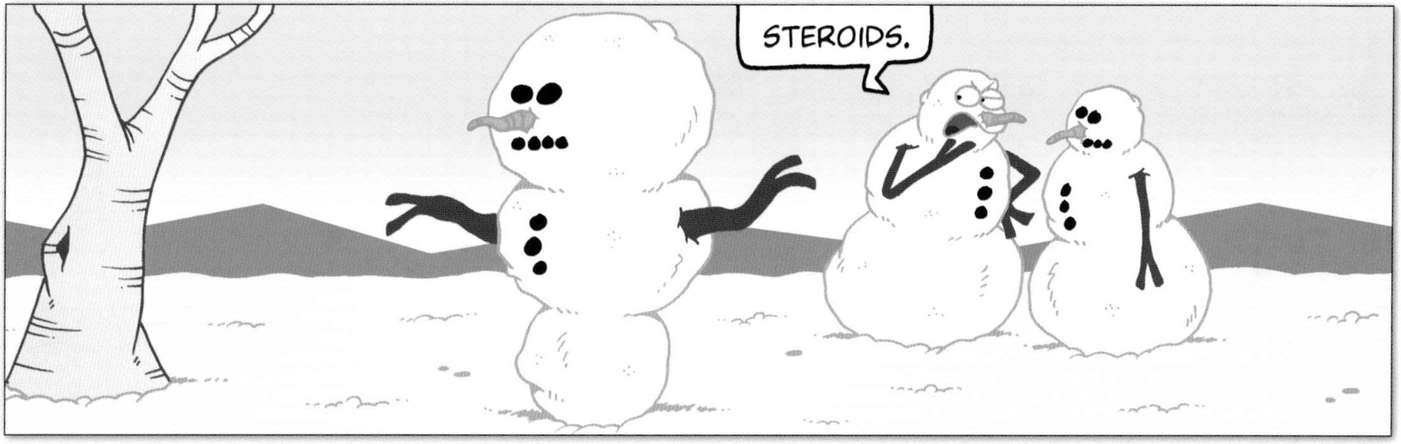
STEROIDS.

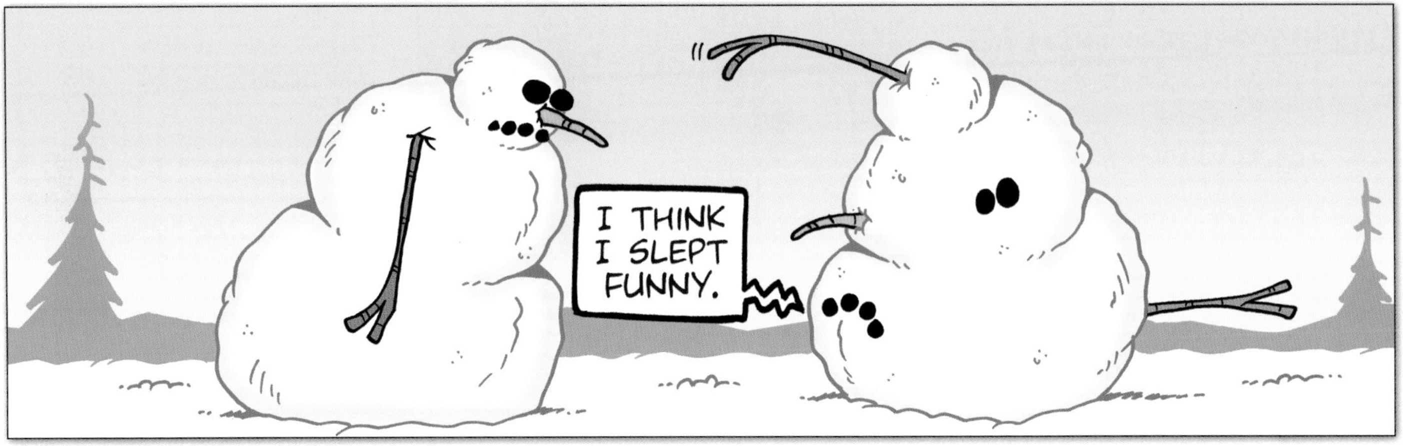
I THINK I SLEPT FUNNY.

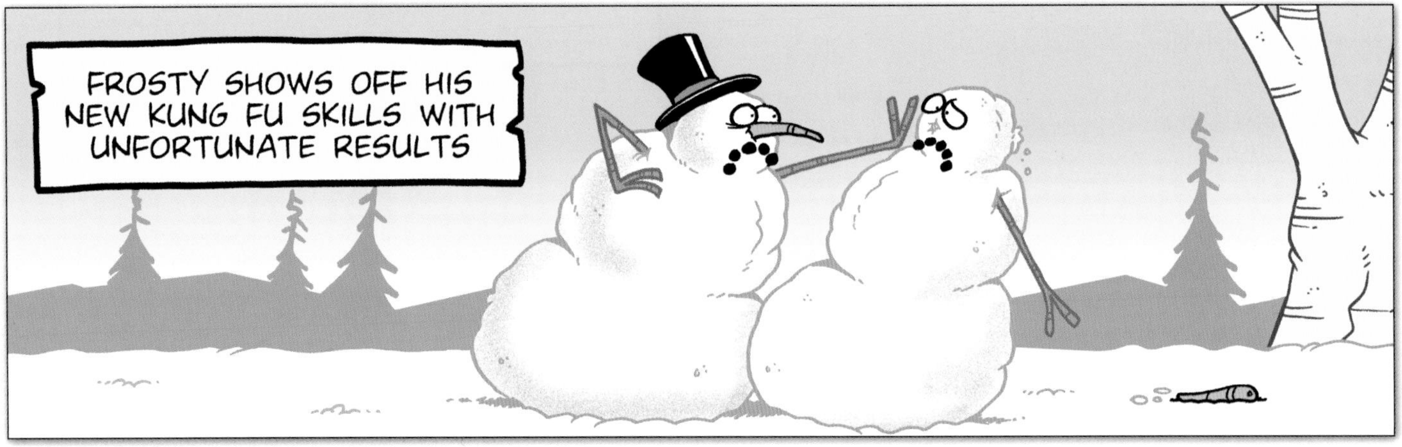
FROSTY SHOWS OFF HIS NEW KUNG FU SKILLS WITH UNFORTUNATE RESULTS

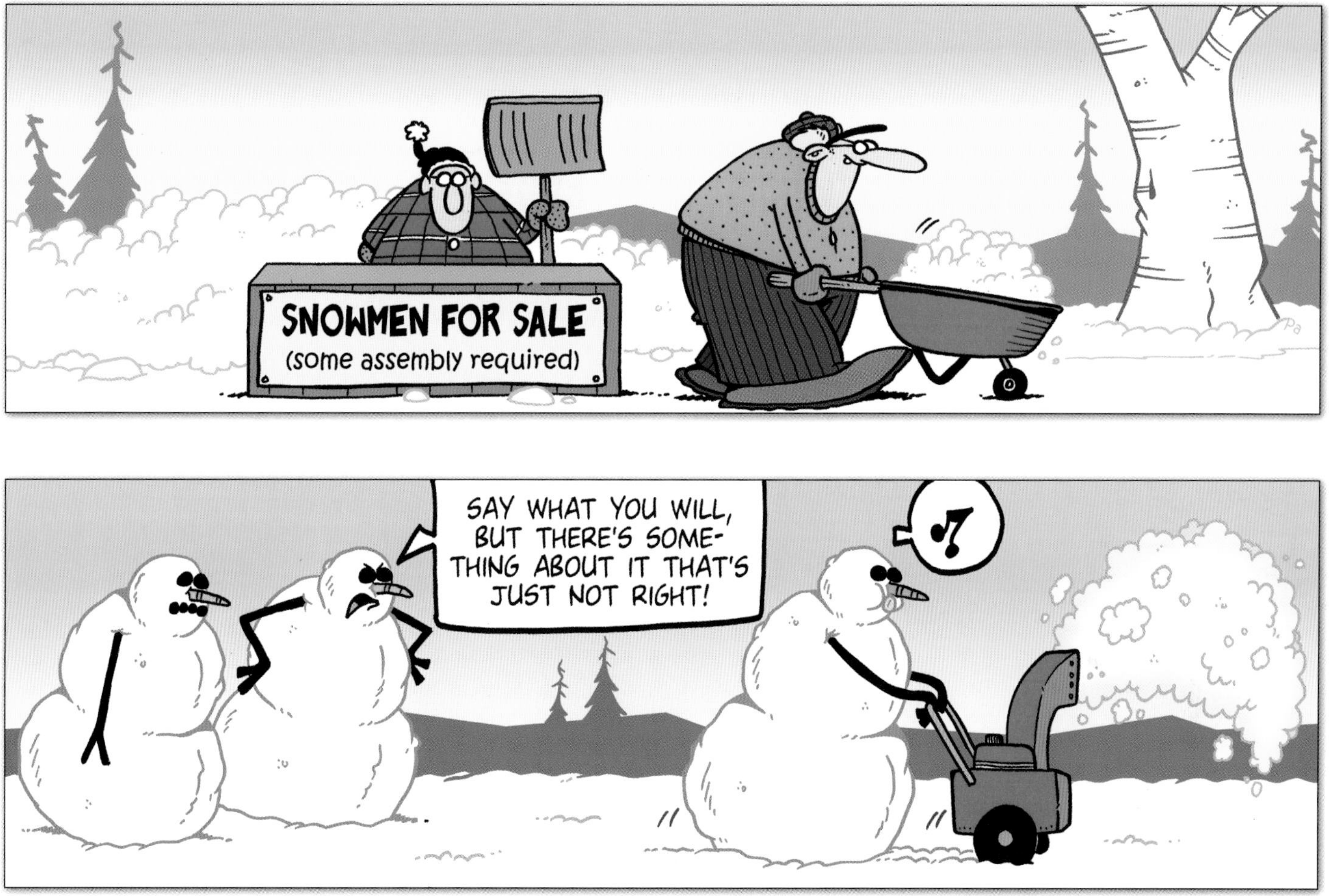
SNOWMEN FOR SALE
(some assembly required)
SAY WHAT YOU WILL, BUT THERE'S SOMETHING ABOUT IT THAT'S JUST NOT RIGHT!

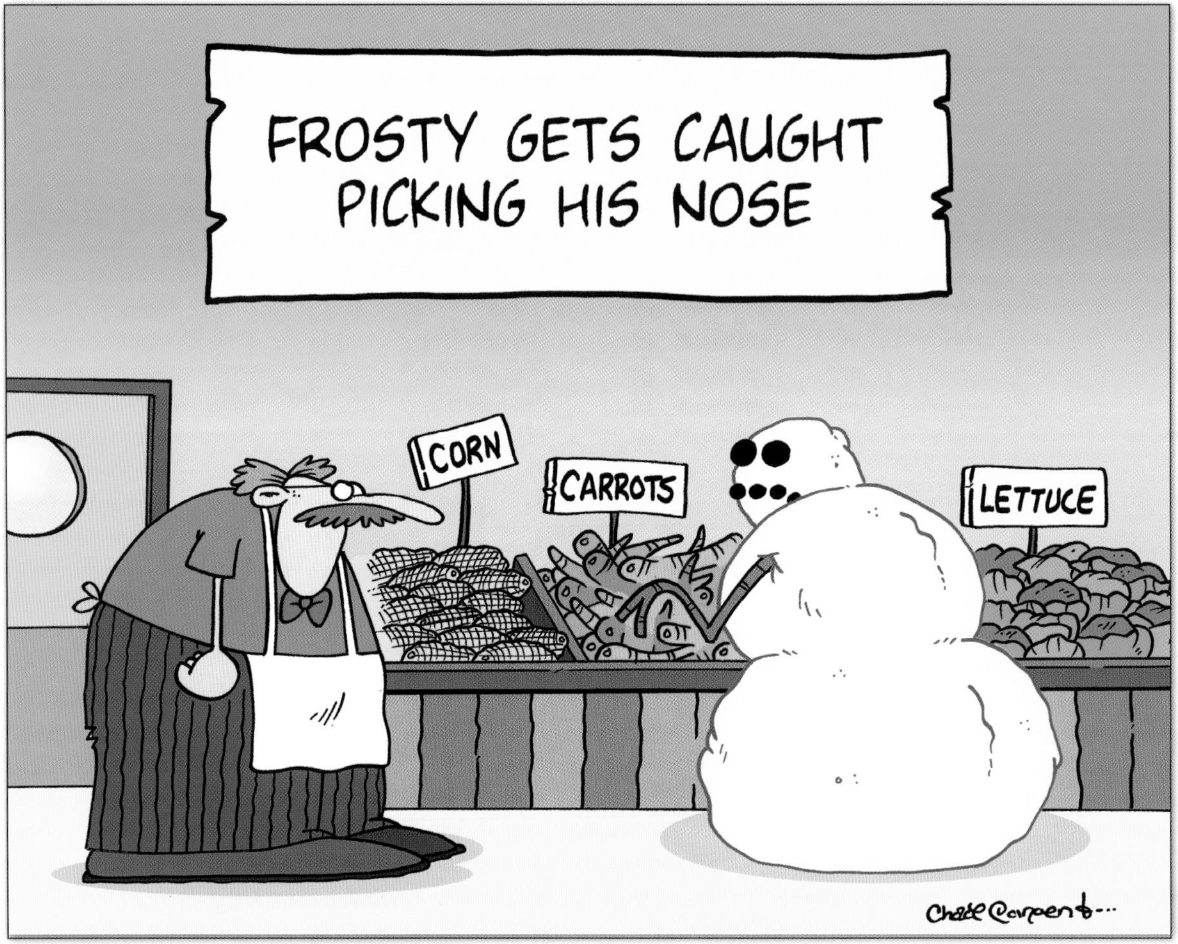
FROSTY GETS CAUGHT PICKING HIS NOSE
CORN
CARROTS
LETTUCE

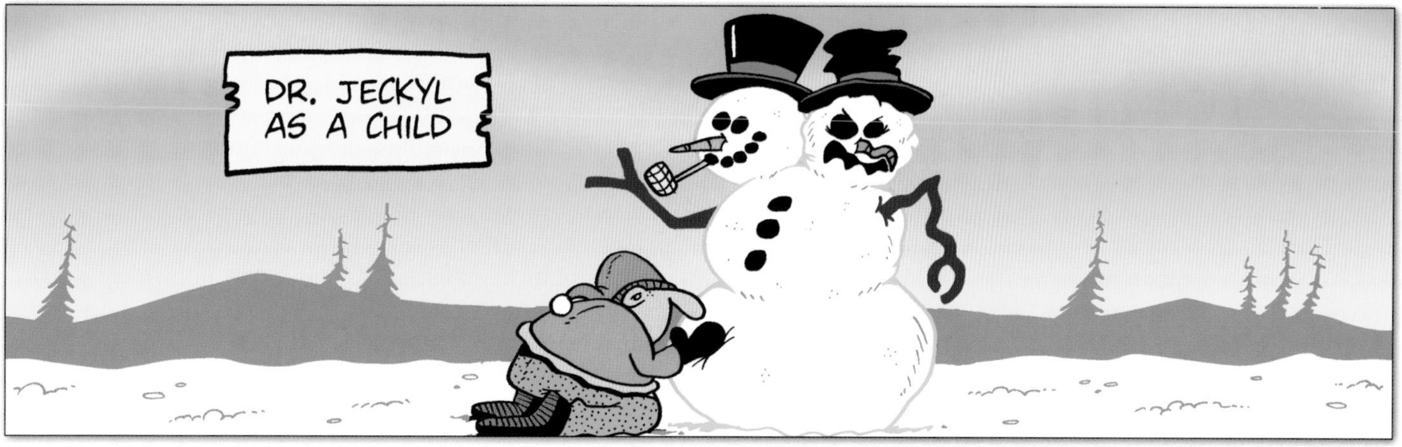
DR. JECKYL
AS A CHILD

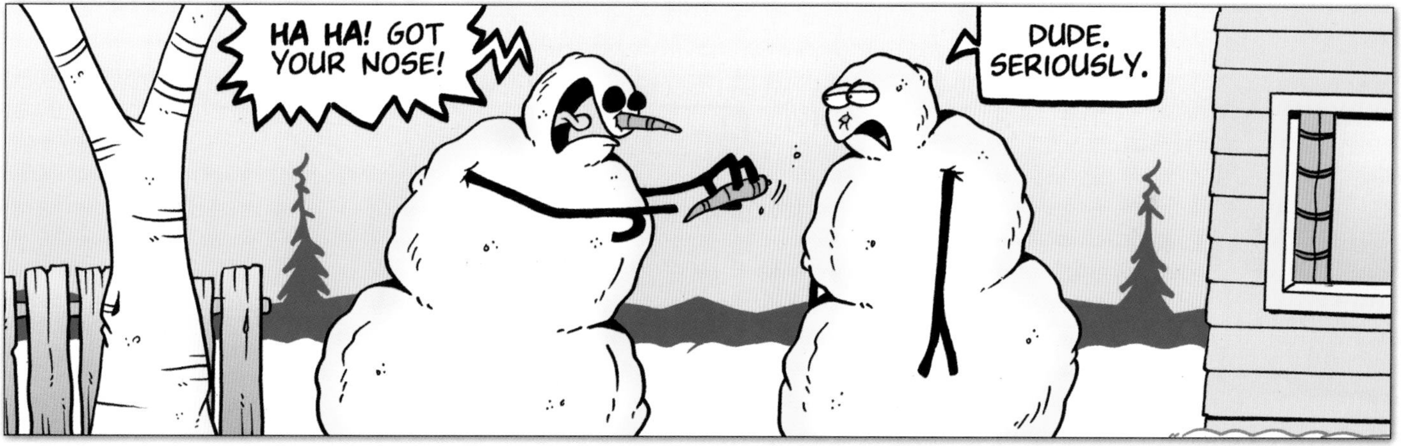
HA HA! GOT YOUR NOSE!
DUDE. SERIOUSLY.

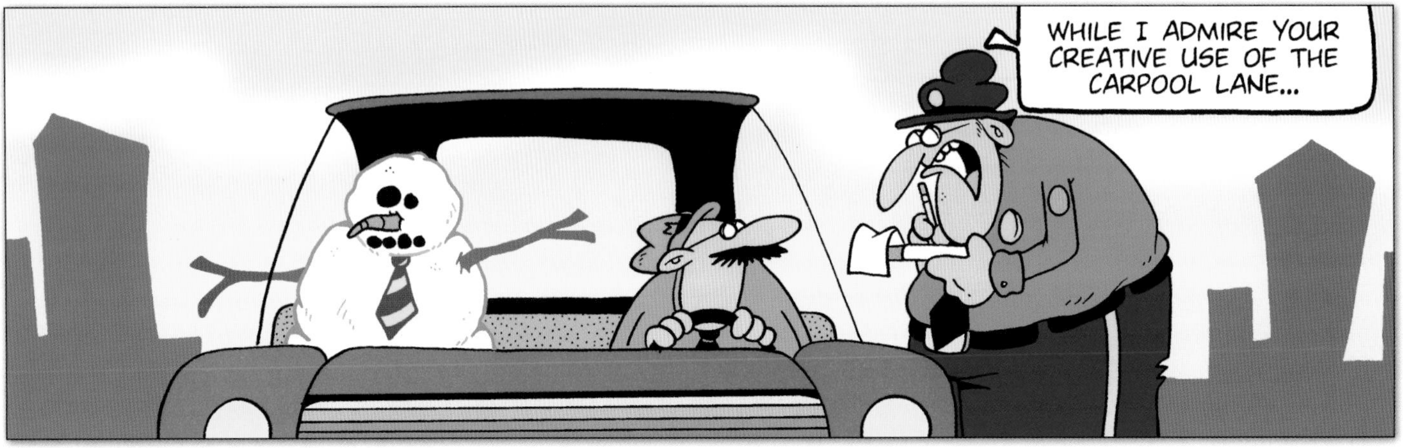
WHILE I ADMIRE YOUR CREATIVE USE OF THE CARPOOL LANE...

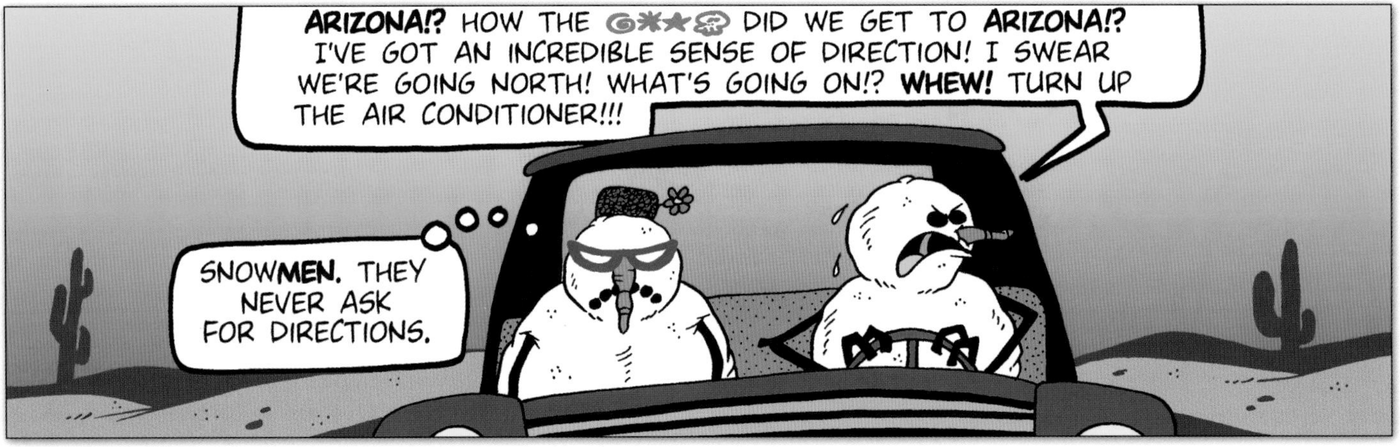
ARIZONA!? HOW THE @*★@ DID WE GET TO ARIZONA!? I'VE GOT AN INCREDIBLE SENSE OF DIRECTION! I SWEAR WE'RE GOING NORTH! WHAT'S GOING ON!? WHEW! TURN UP THE AIR CONDITIONER!!!
SNOWMEN. THEY NEVER ASK FOR DIRECTIONS.

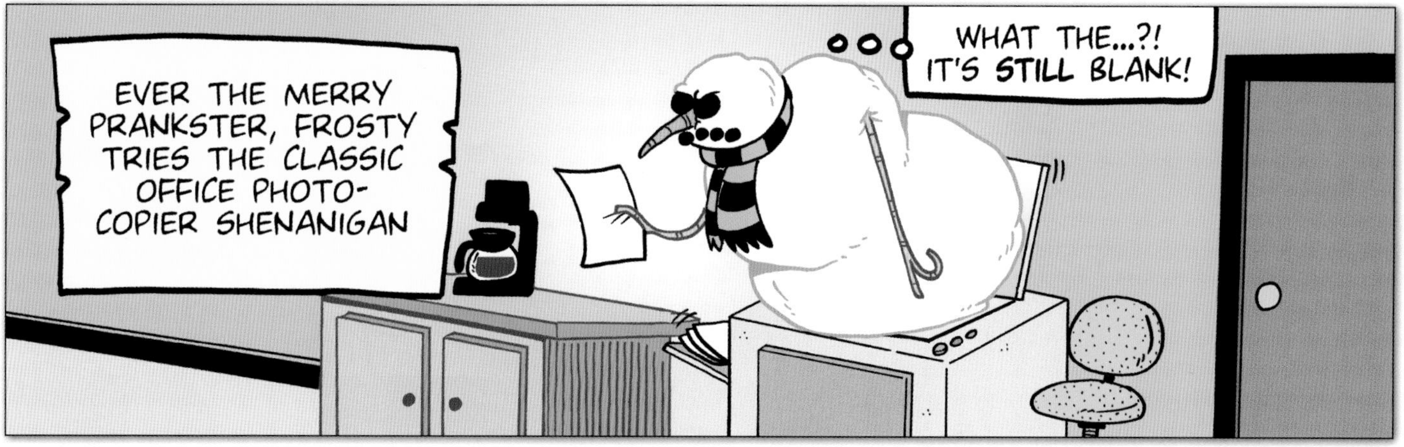
EVER THE MERRY PRANKSTER, FROSTY TRIES THE CLASSIC OFFICE PHOTO-COPIER SHENANIGAN
WHAT THE...?! IT'S STILL BLANK!

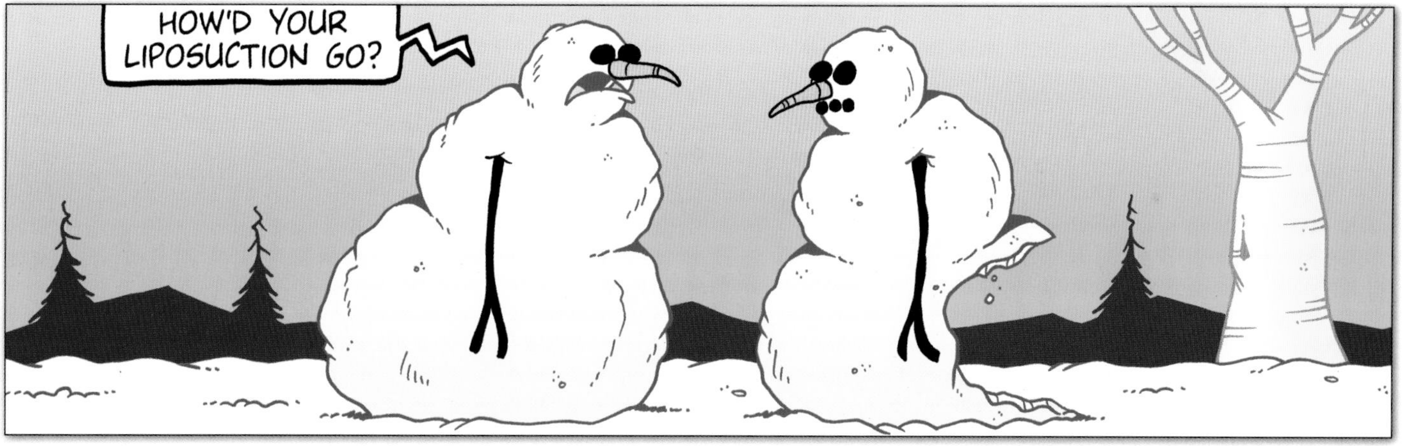
HOW'D YOUR LIPOSUCTION GO?

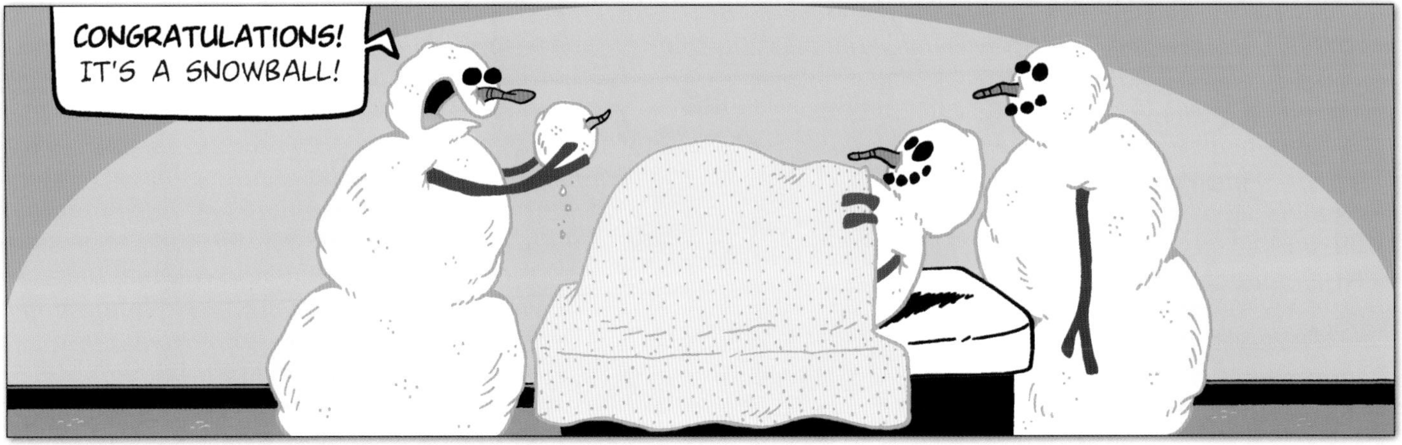
CONGRATULATIONS!
IT'S A SNOWBALL!

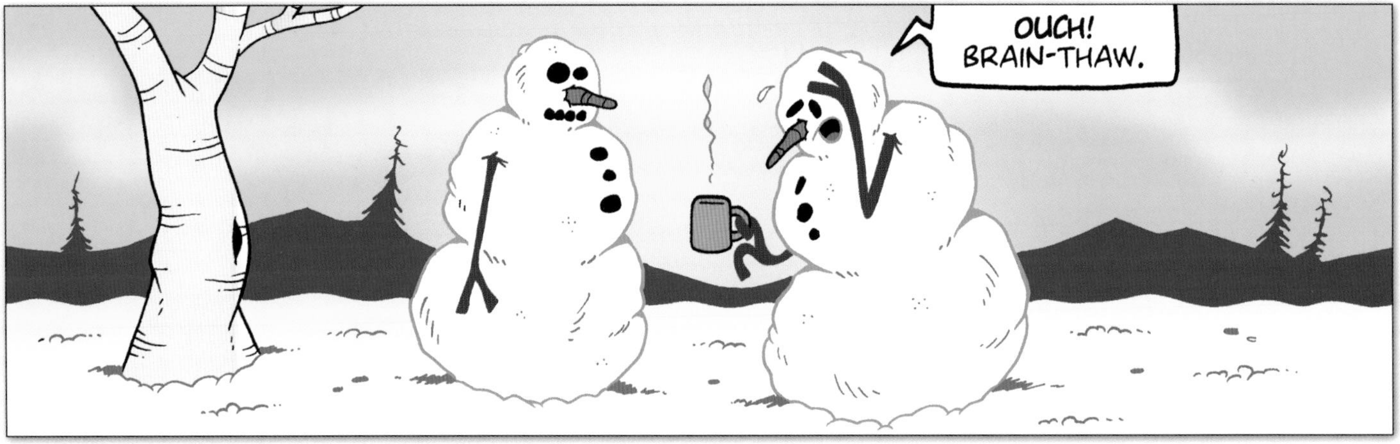
OUCH!
BRAIN-THAW.

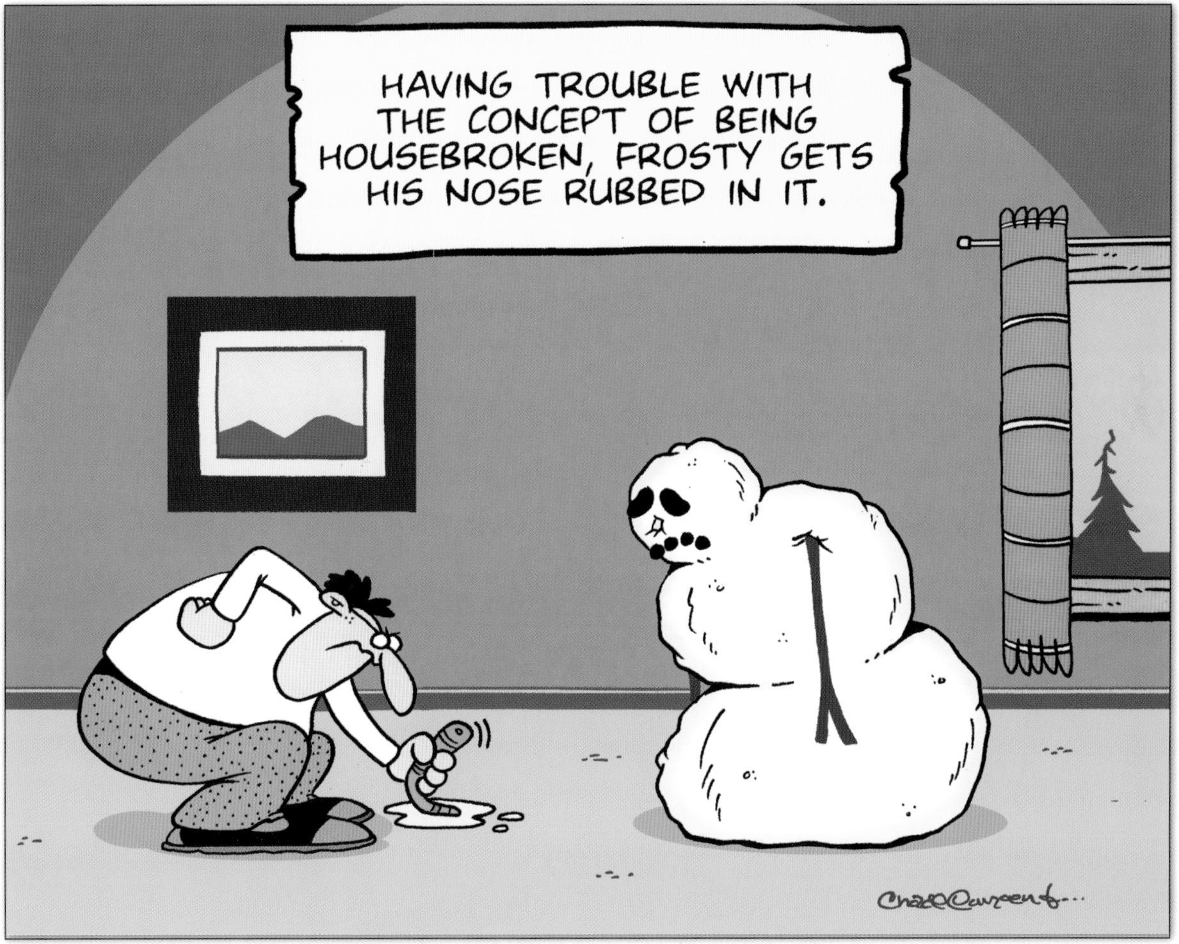
HAVING TROUBLE WITH THE CONCEPT OF BEING HOUSEBROKEN, FROSTY GETS HIS NOSE RUBBED IN IT.

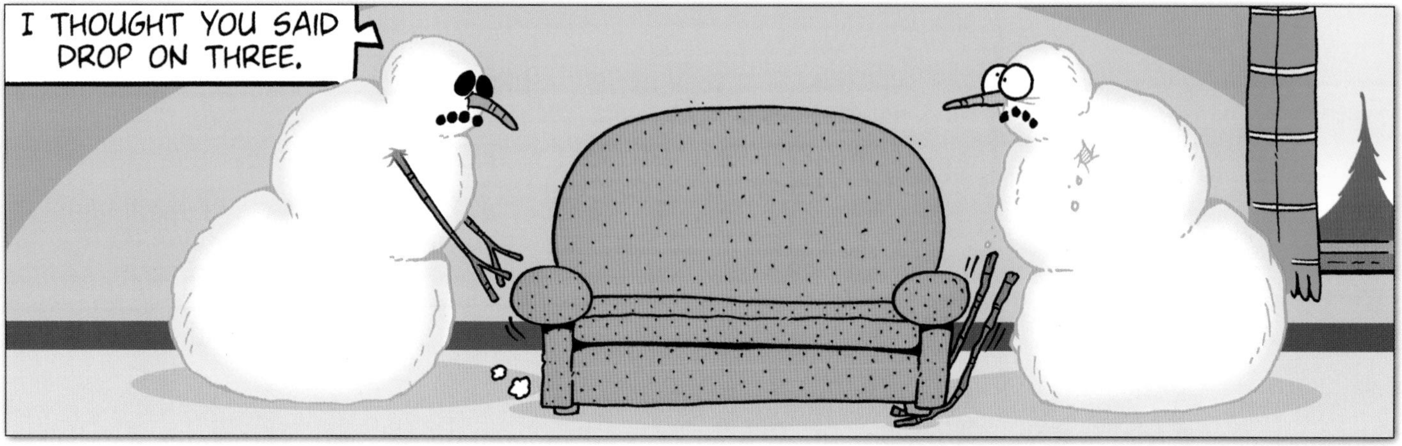
I THOUGHT YOU SAID DROP ON THREE.

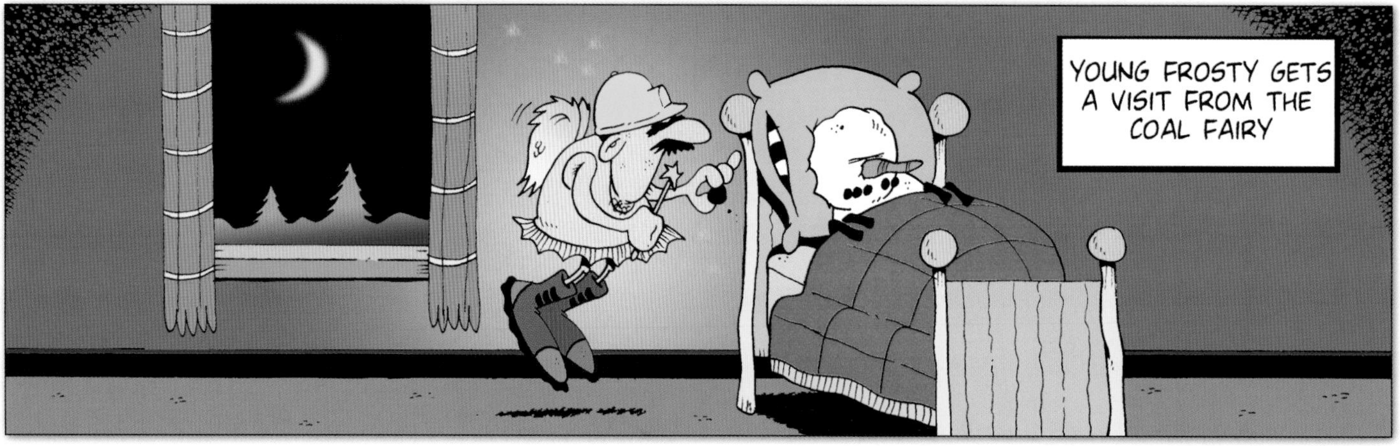
YOUNG FROSTY GETS A VISIT FROM THE COAL FAIRY

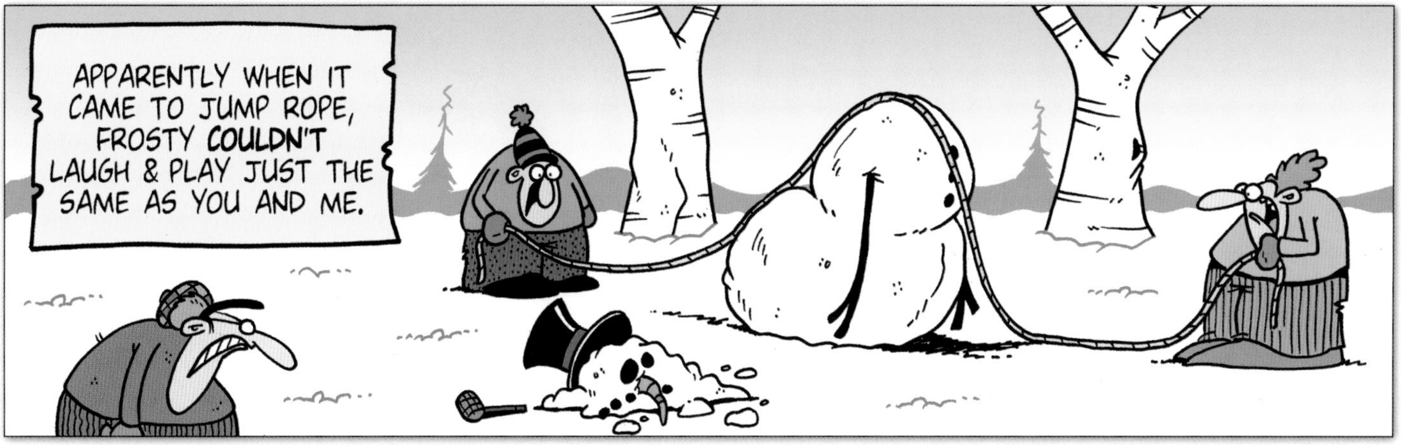
APPARENTLY WHEN IT CAME TO JUMP ROPE, FROSTY **COULDN'T** LAUGH & PLAY JUST THE SAME AS YOU AND ME.

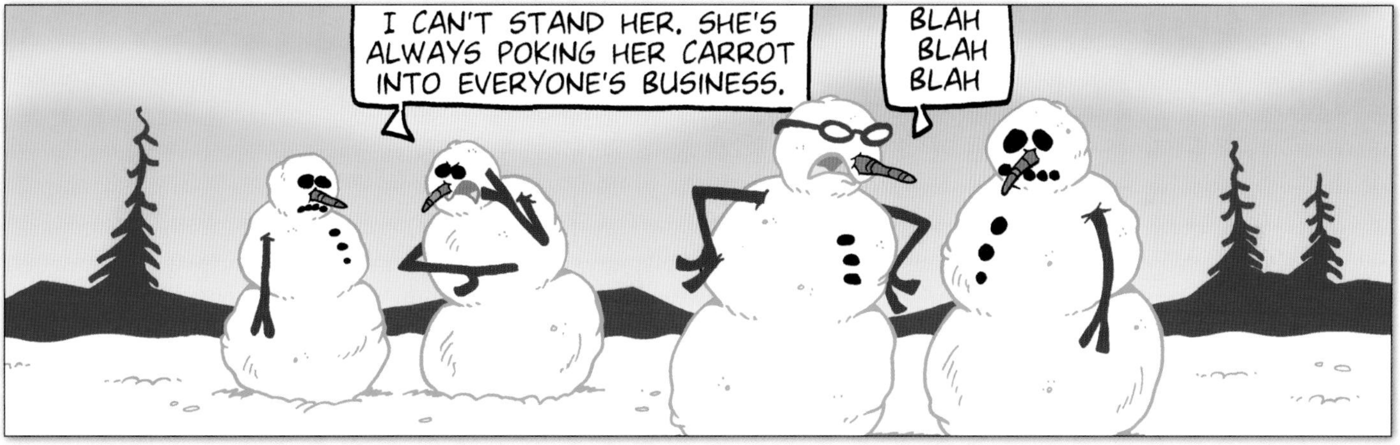
I CAN'T STAND HER. SHE'S ALWAYS POKING HER CARROT INTO EVERYONE'S BUSINESS.
BLAH BLAH BLAH

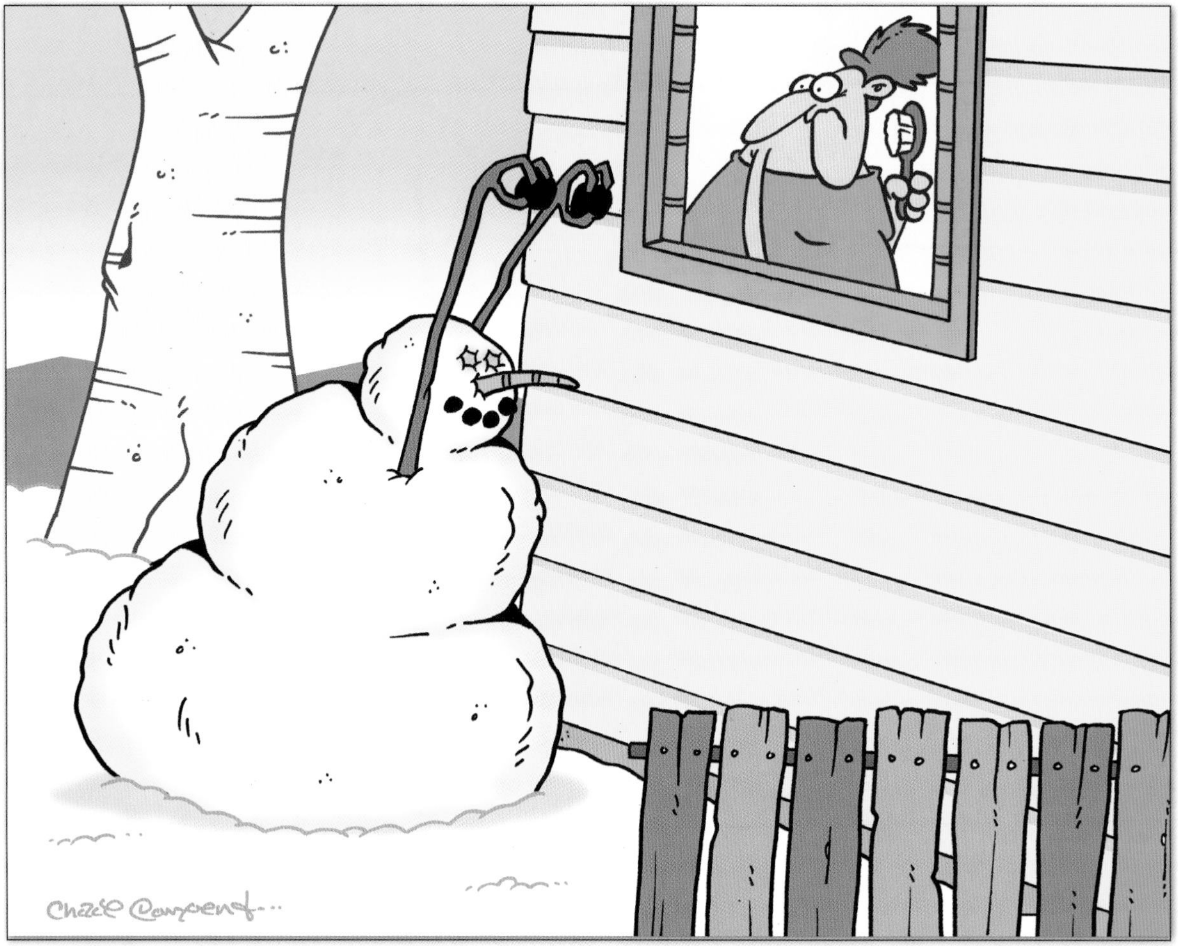

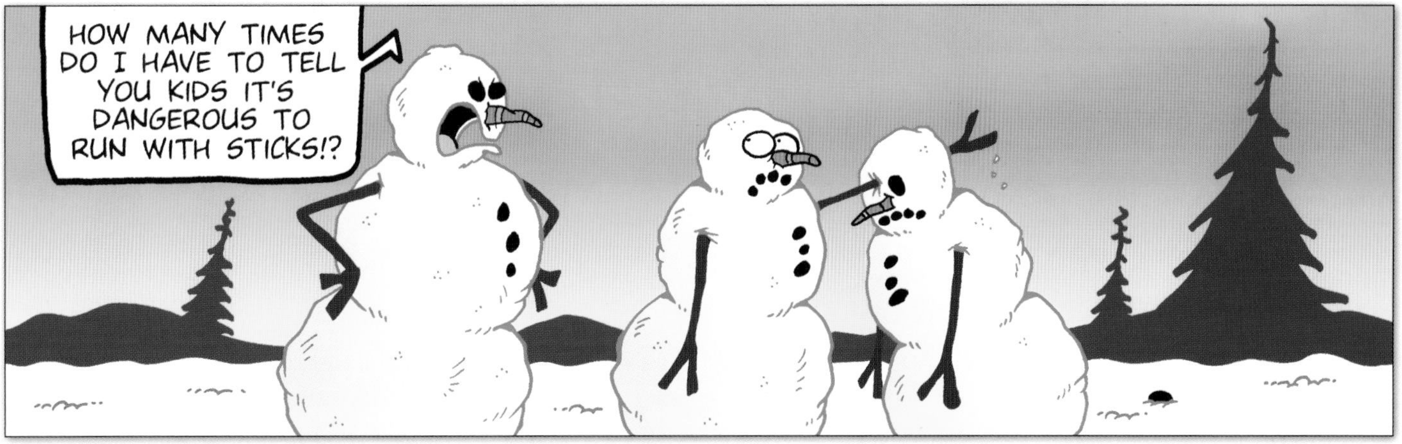
HOW MANY TIMES DO I HAVE TO TELL YOU KIDS IT'S DANGEROUS TO RUN WITH STICKS!?

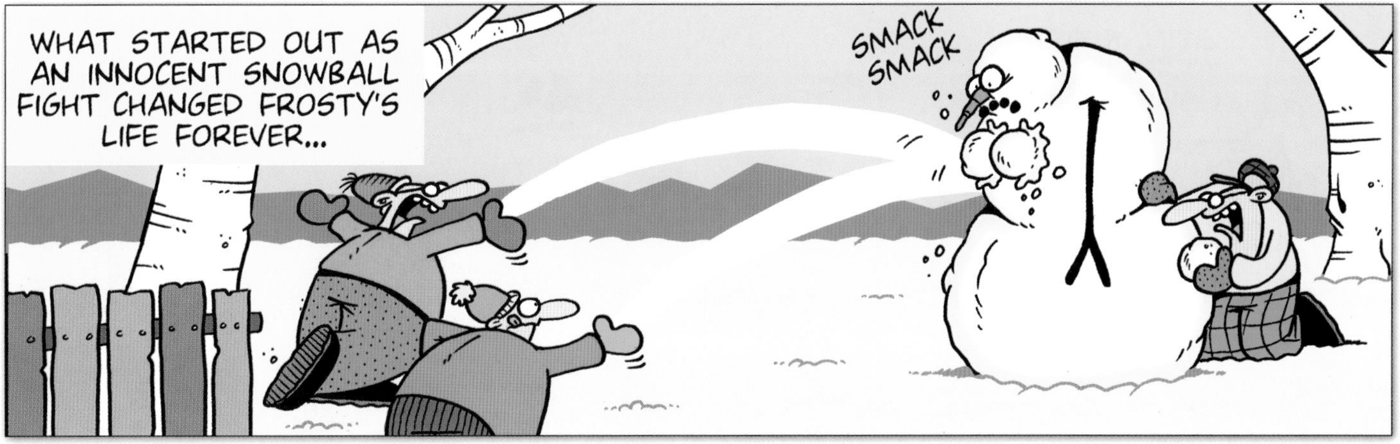
WHAT STARTED OUT AS AN INNOCENT SNOWBALL FIGHT CHANGED FROSTY'S LIFE FOREVER...
SMACK
SMACK

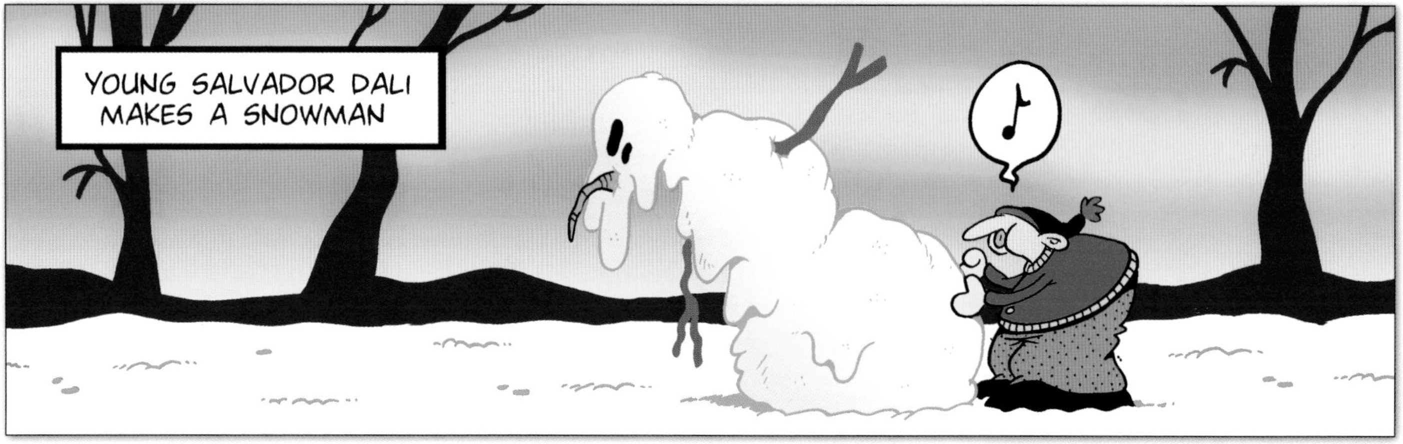
YOUNG SALVADOR DALI MAKES A SNOWMAN

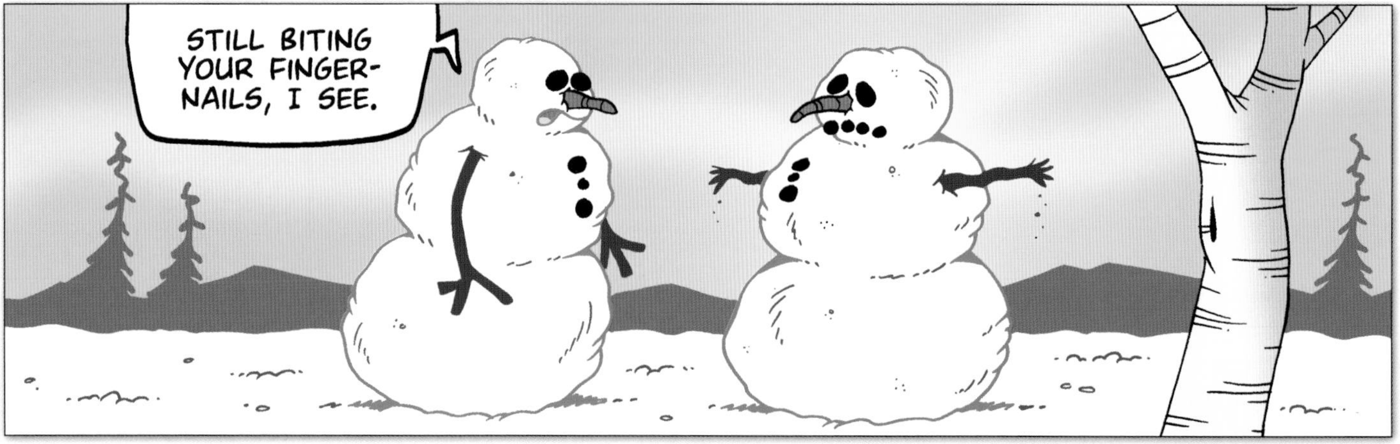
STILL BITING YOUR FINGER-NAILS, I SEE.

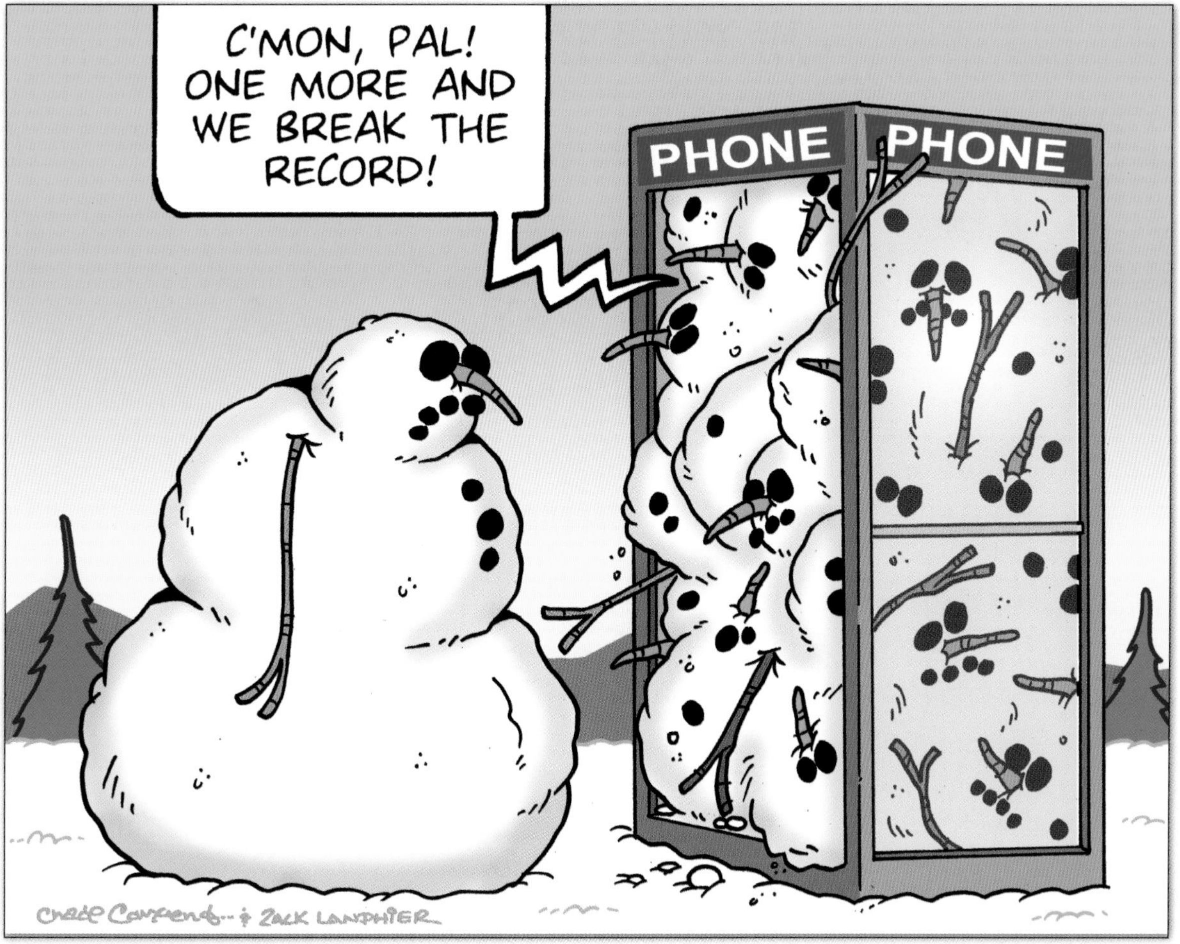
C'MON, PAL! ONE MORE AND WE BREAK THE RECORD!
PHONE
PHONE

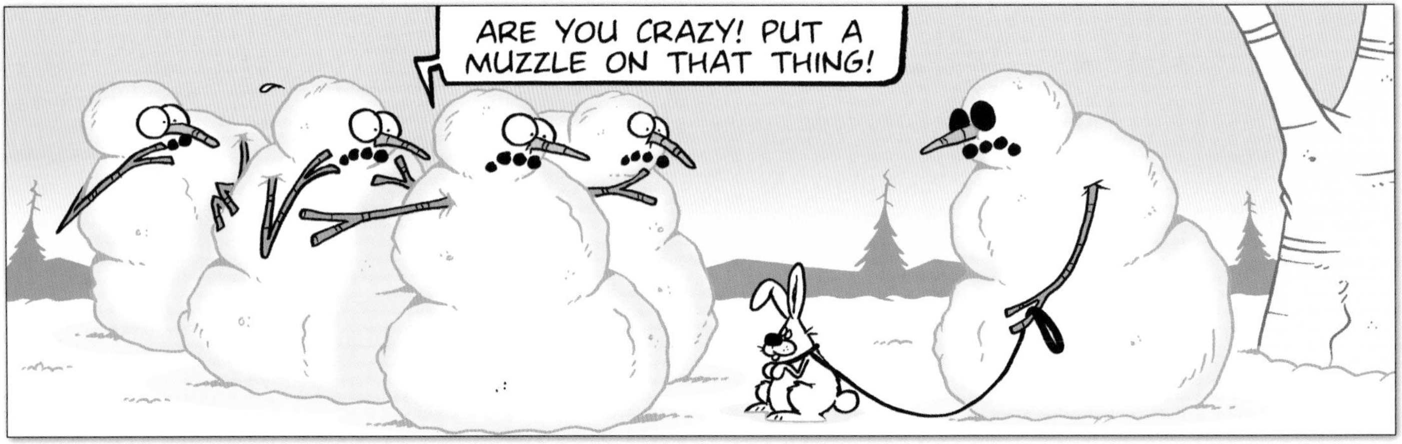
ARE YOU CRAZY! PUT A MUZZLE ON THAT THING!

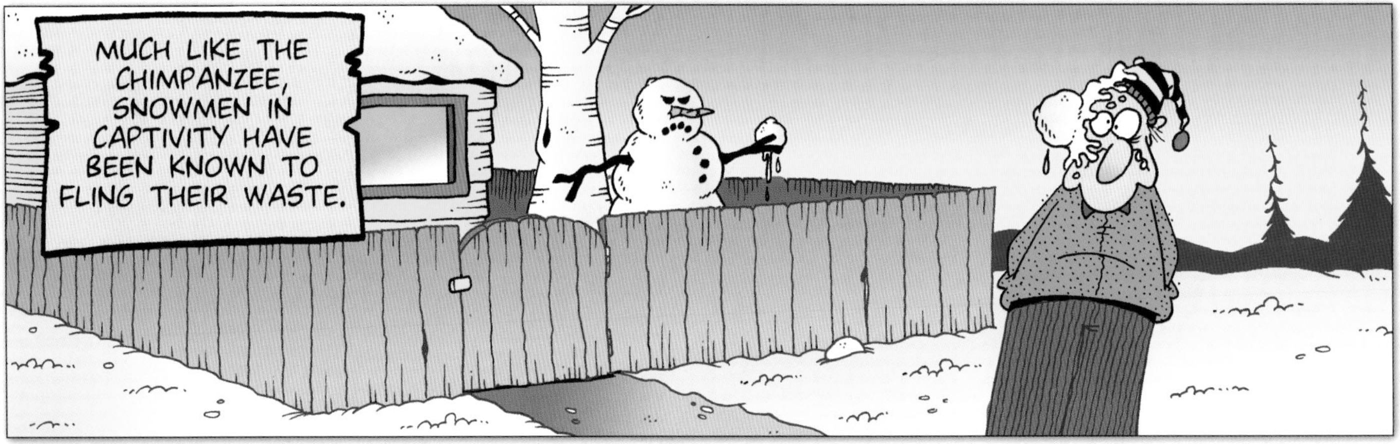
MUCH LIKE THE CHIMPANZEE, SNOWMEN IN CAPTIVITY HAVE BEEN KNOWN TO FLING THEIR WASTE.

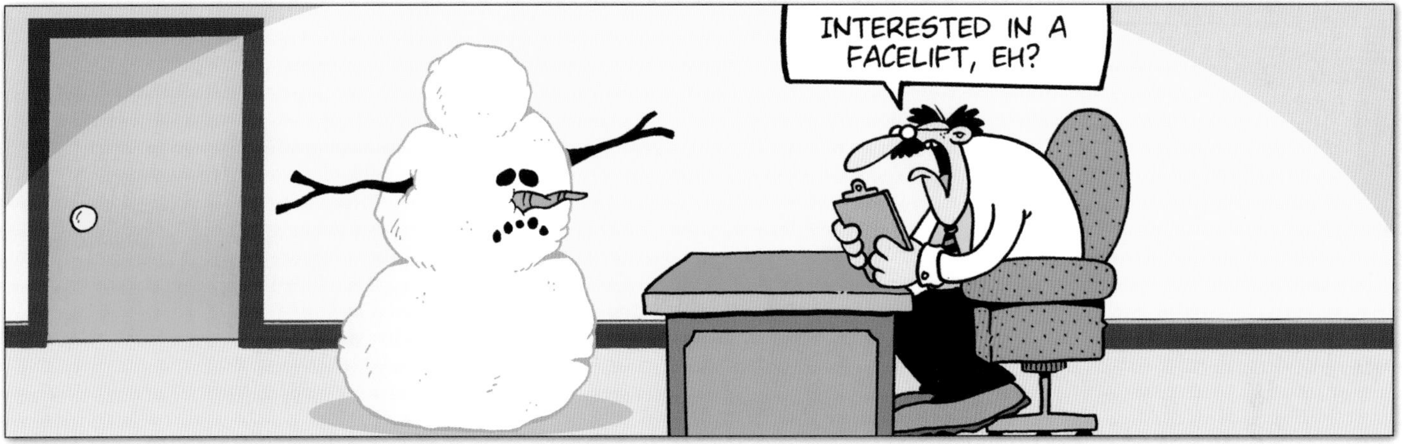
INTERESTED IN A FACELIFT, EH?

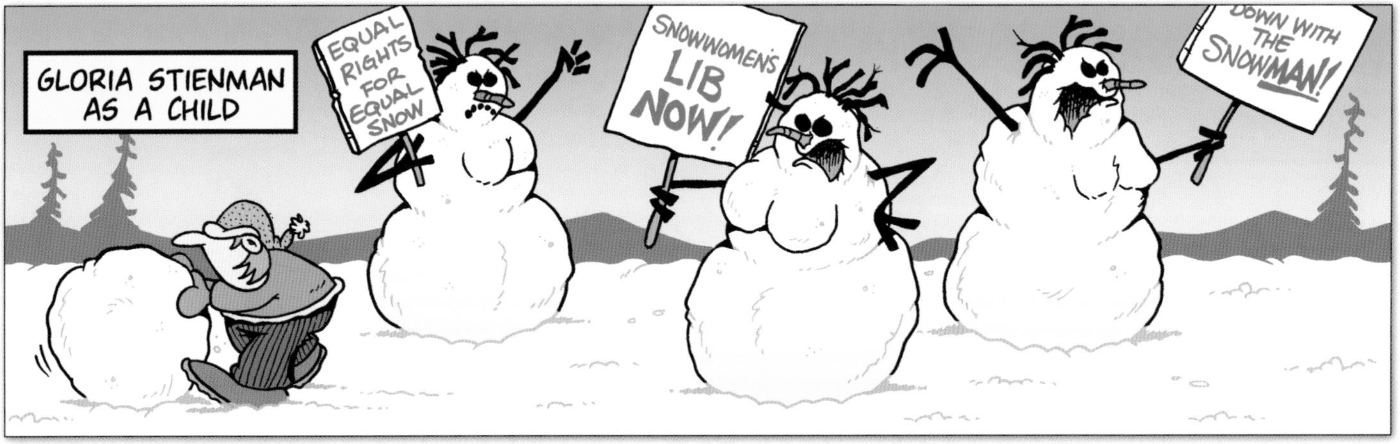
GLORIA STIENMAN AS A CHILD
EQUAL RIGHTS FOR EQUAL SNOW
SNOWWOMEN'S LIB NOW!
DOWN WITH THE SNOWMAN!

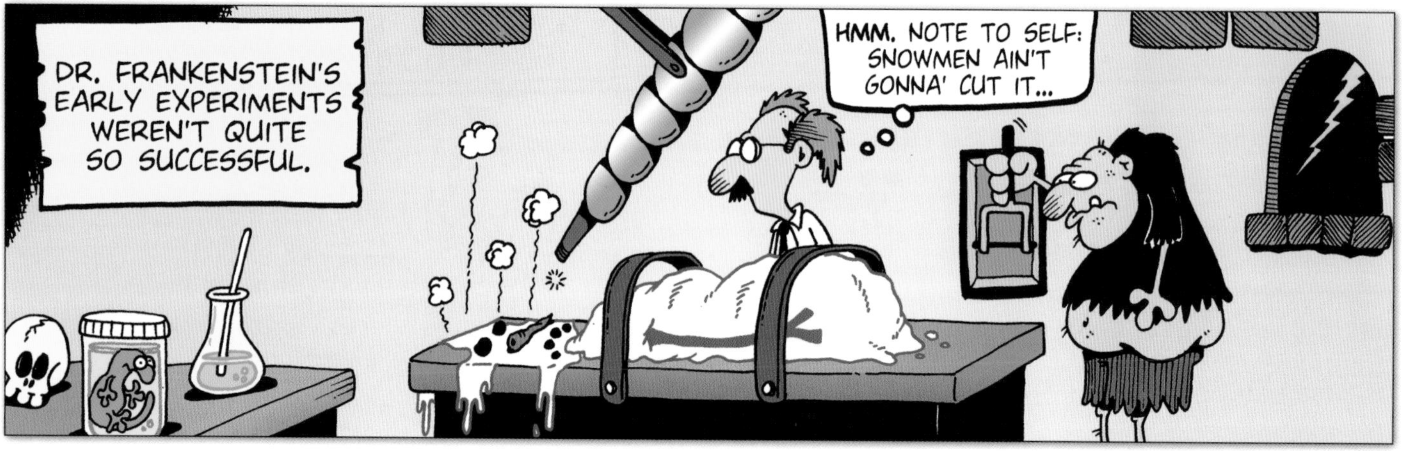
DR. FRANKENSTEIN'S EARLY EXPERIMENTS WEREN'T QUITE SO SUCCESSFUL.
HMM. NOTE TO SELF: SNOWMEN AIN'T GONNA' CUT IT...

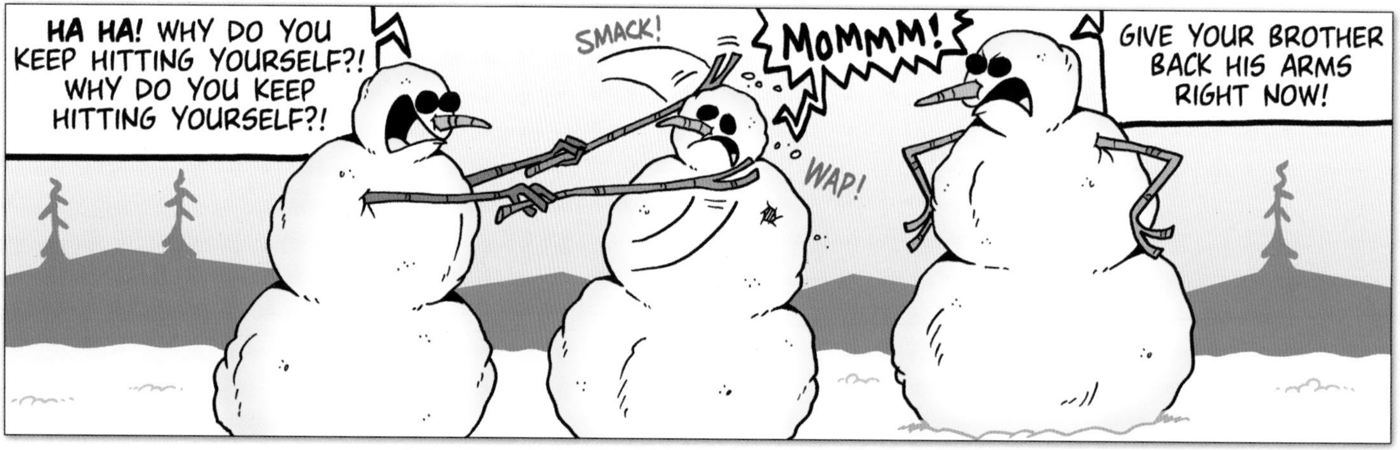
HA HA! WHY DO YOU KEEP HITTING YOURSELF?! WHY DO YOU KEEP HITTING YOURSELF?!
SMACK!
MOMMM!
WAP!
GIVE YOUR BROTHER BACK HIS ARMS RIGHT NOW!

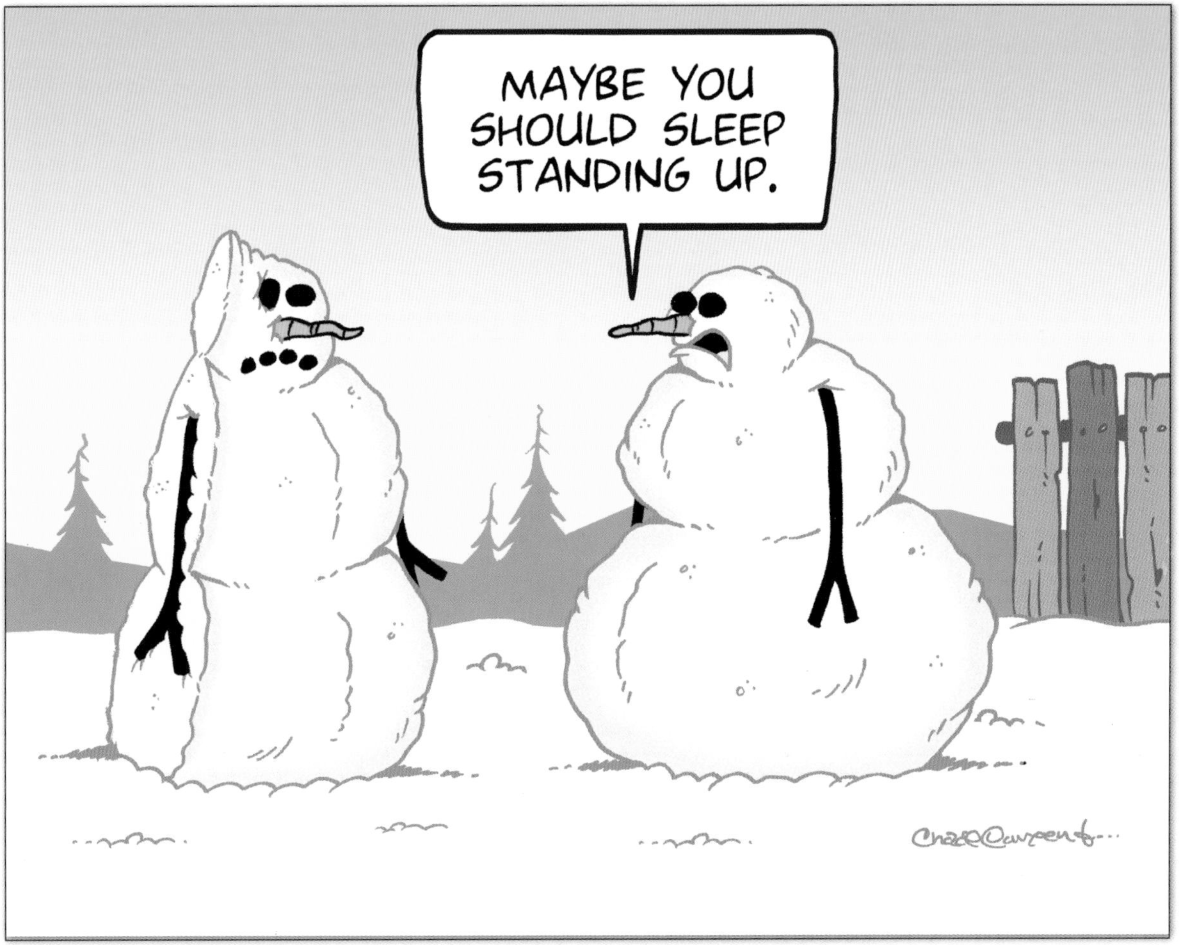
MAYBE YOU SHOULD SLEEP STANDING UP.
Chad Carpenter

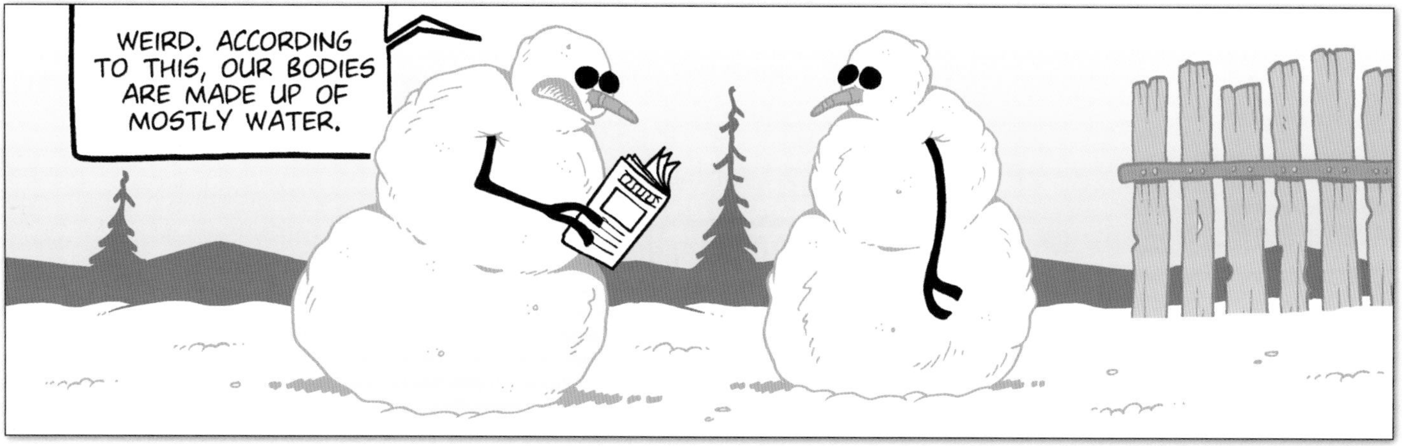
WEIRD. ACCORDING TO THIS, OUR BODIES ARE MADE UP OF MOSTLY WATER.

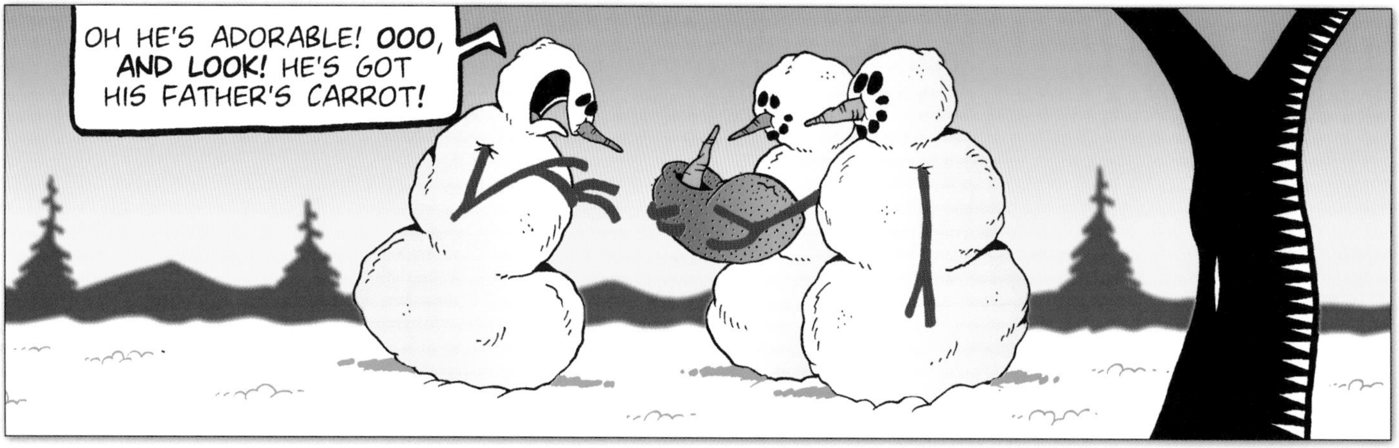
OH HE'S ADORABLE! **OOO, AND LOOK!** HE'S GOT HIS FATHER'S CARROT!

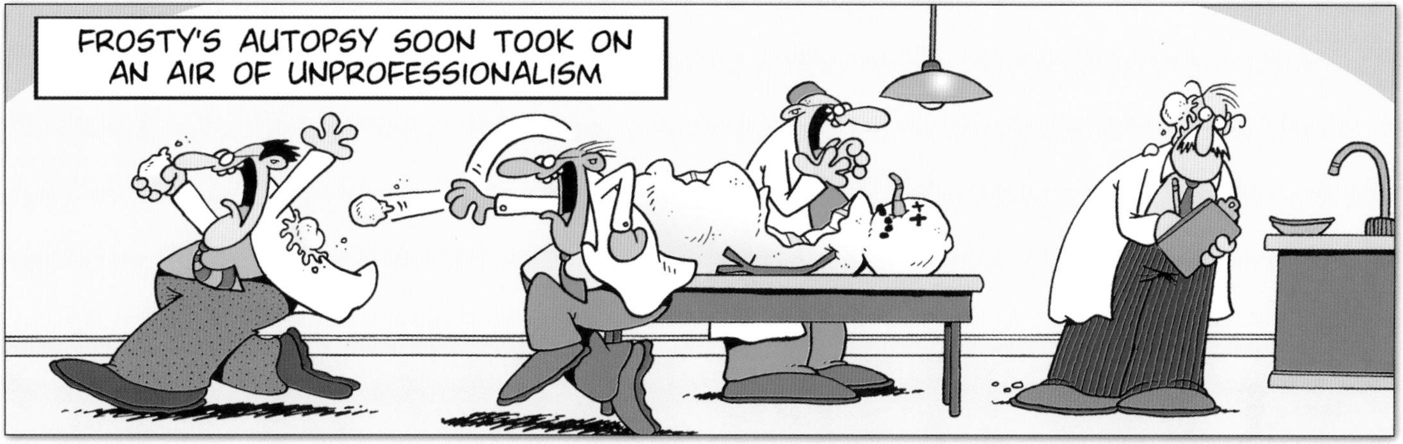
FROSTY'S AUTOPSY SOON TOOK ON AN AIR OF UNPROFESSIONALISM

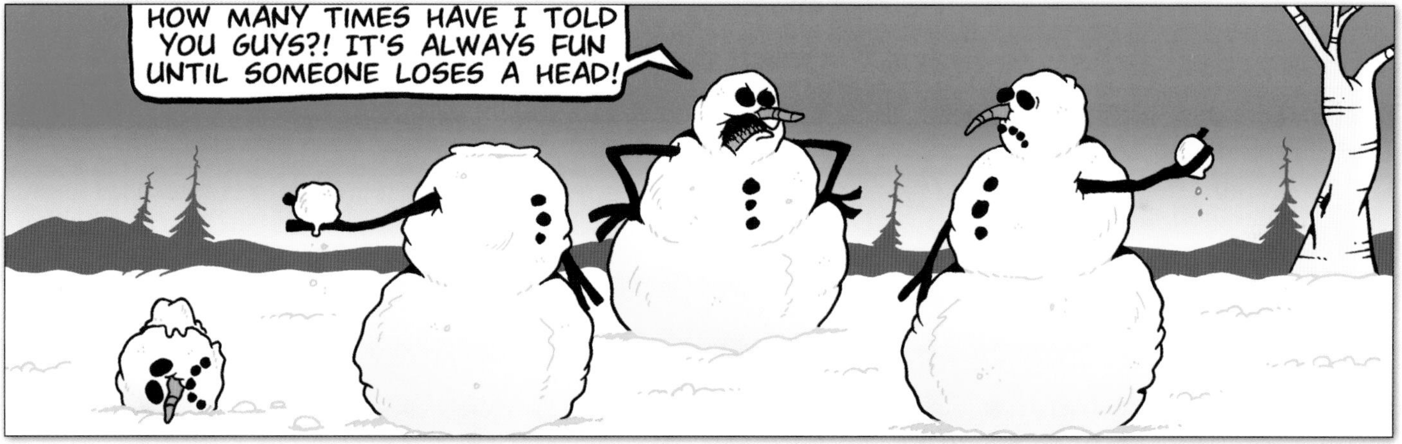
HOW MANY TIMES HAVE I TOLD YOU GUYS?! IT'S ALWAYS FUN UNTIL SOMEONE LOSES A HEAD!

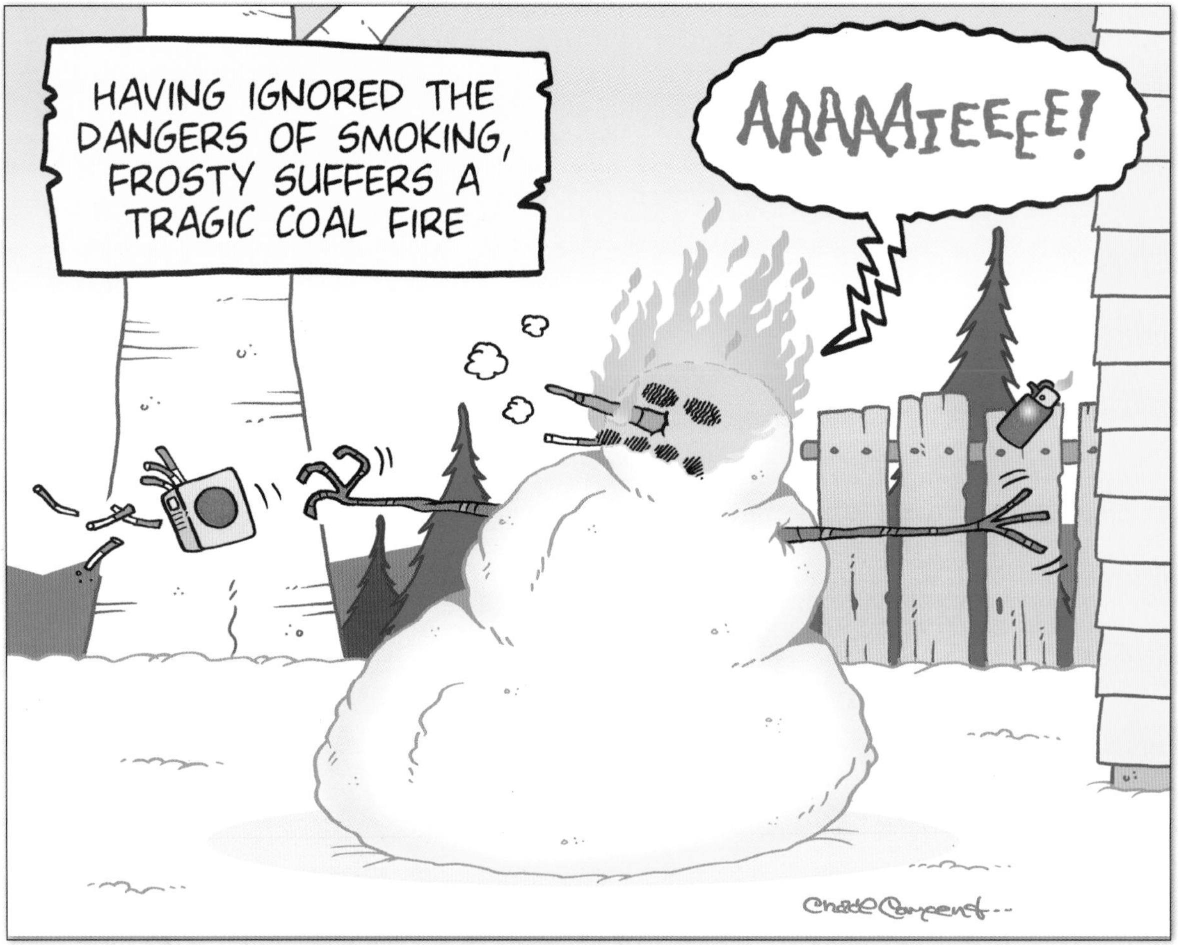
HAVING IGNORED THE DANGERS OF SMOKING, FROSTY SUFFERS A TRAGIC COAL FIRE
AAAAAIEEEEE!

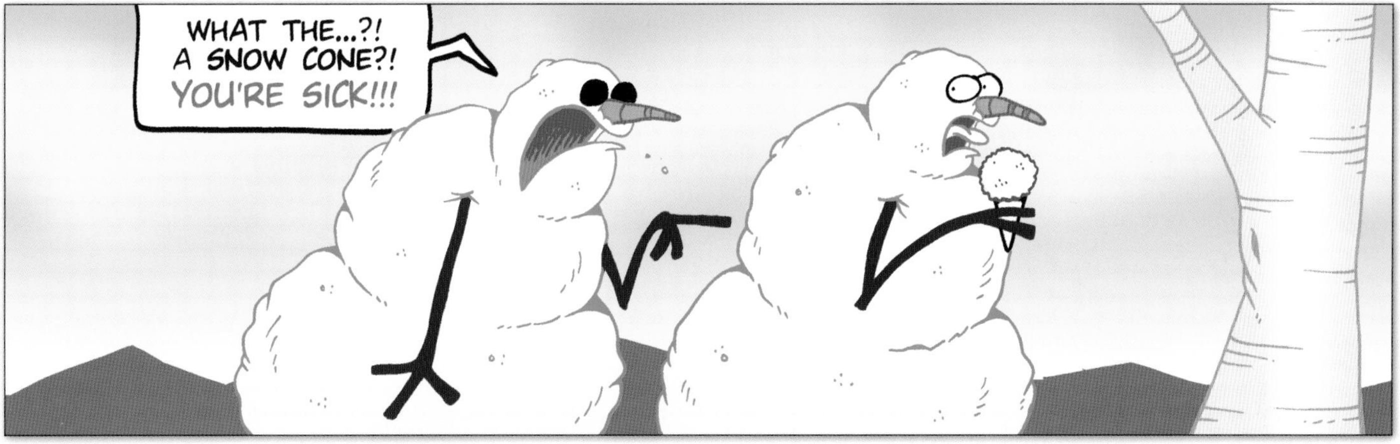
WHAT THE...?! A SNOW CONE?! YOU'RE SICK!!!

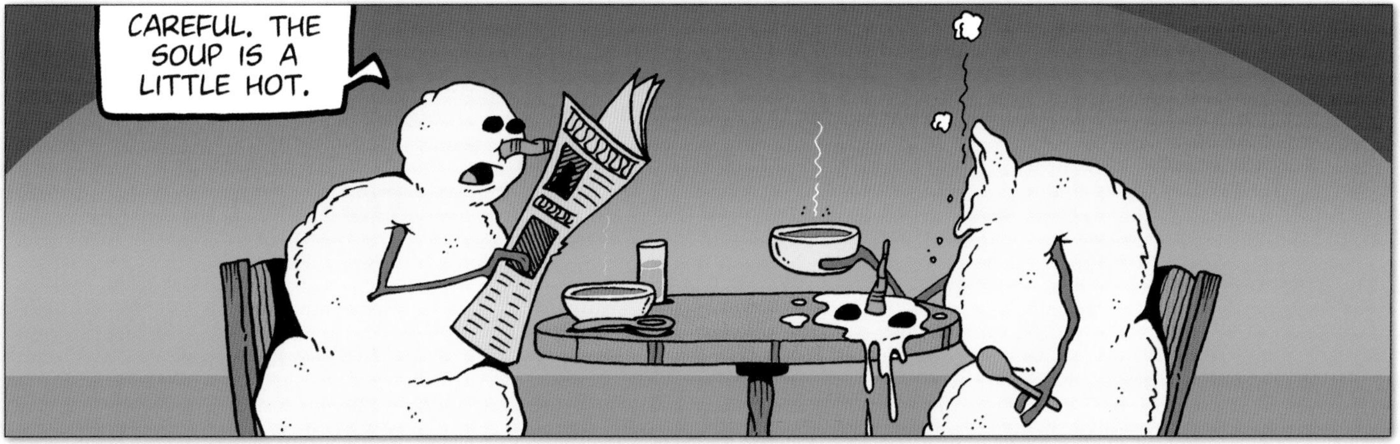
CAREFUL. THE SOUP IS A LITTLE HOT.

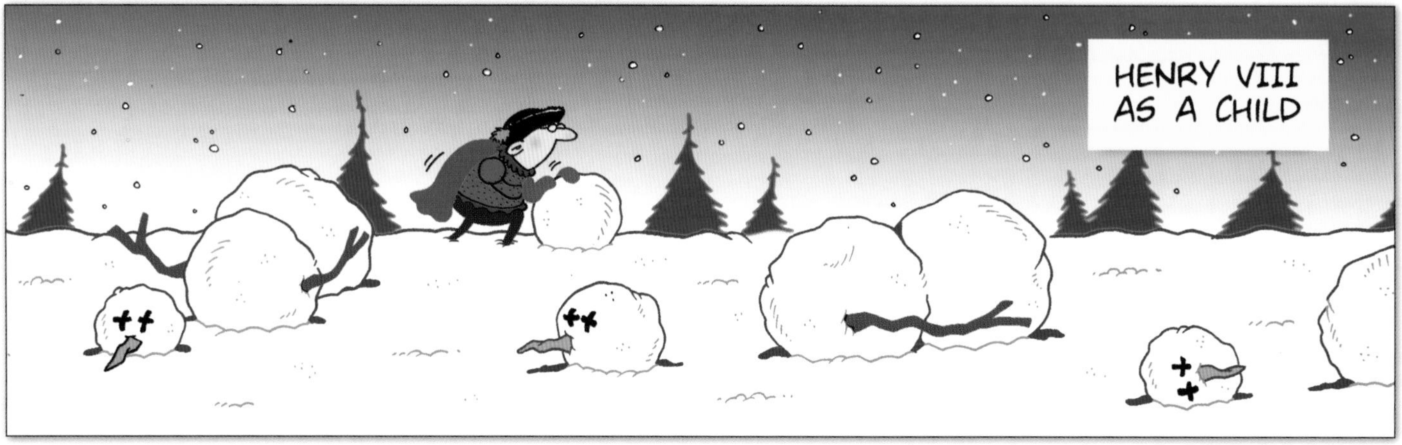
HENRY VIII
AS A CHILD

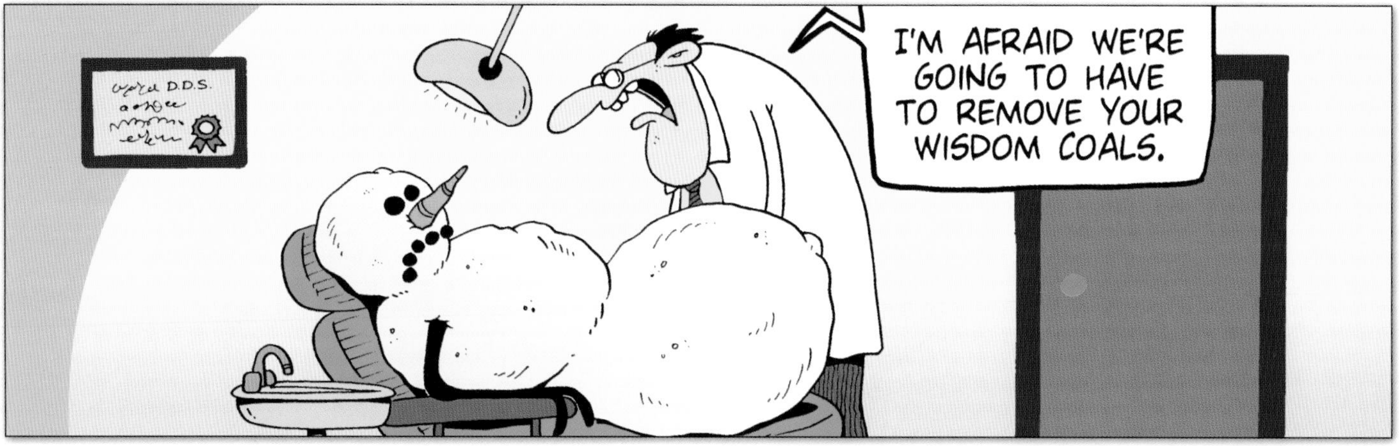
I'M AFRAID WE'RE GOING TO HAVE TO REMOVE YOUR WISDOM COALS.

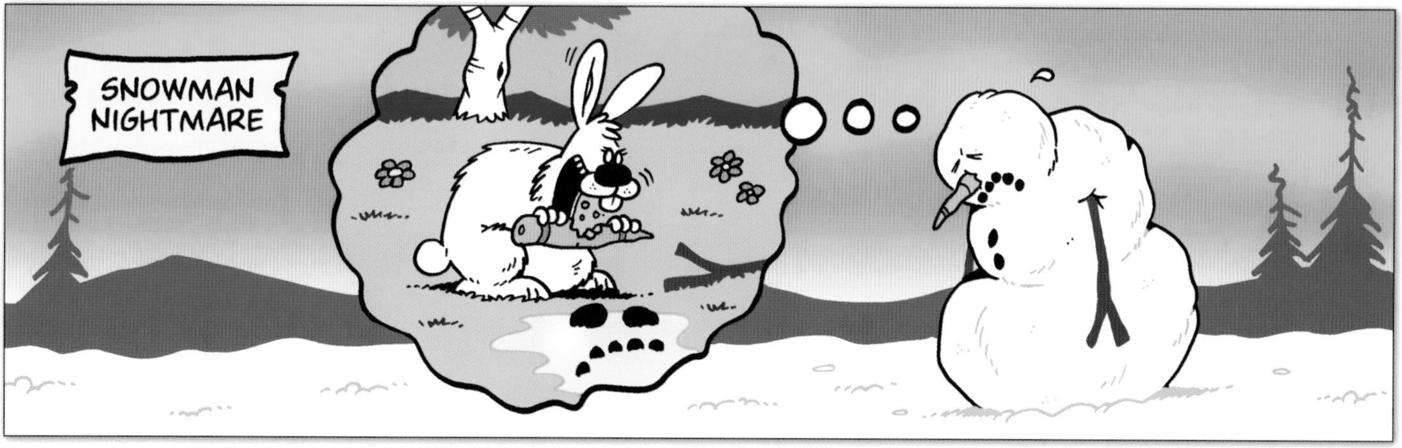
SNOWMAN
NIGHTMARE

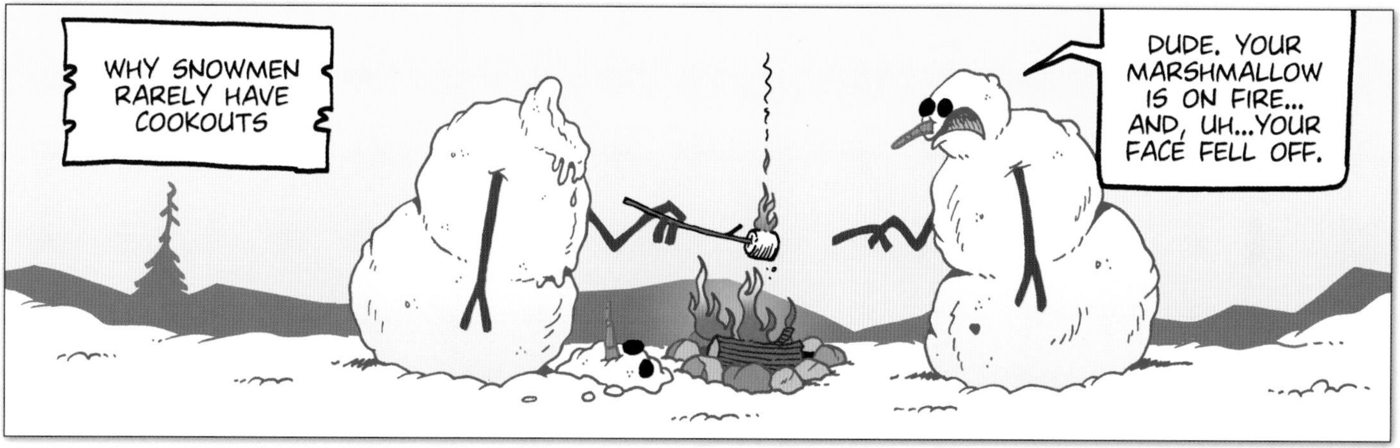
WHY SNOWMEN
RARELY HAVE
COOKOUTS
DUDE. YOUR MARSHMALLOW IS ON FIRE... AND, UH...YOUR FACE FELL OFF.

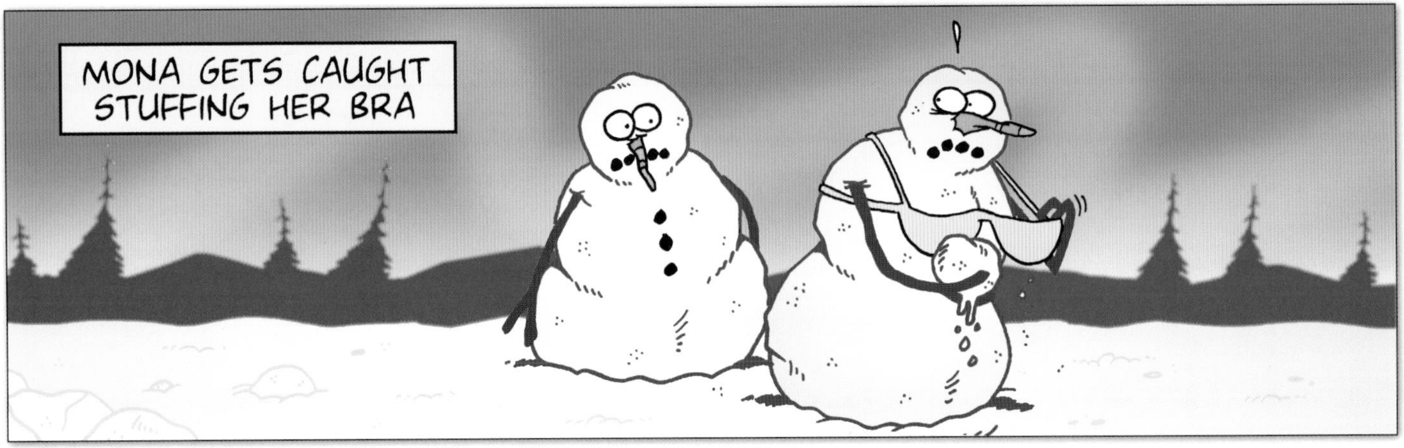
MONA GETS CAUGHT STUFFING HER BRA

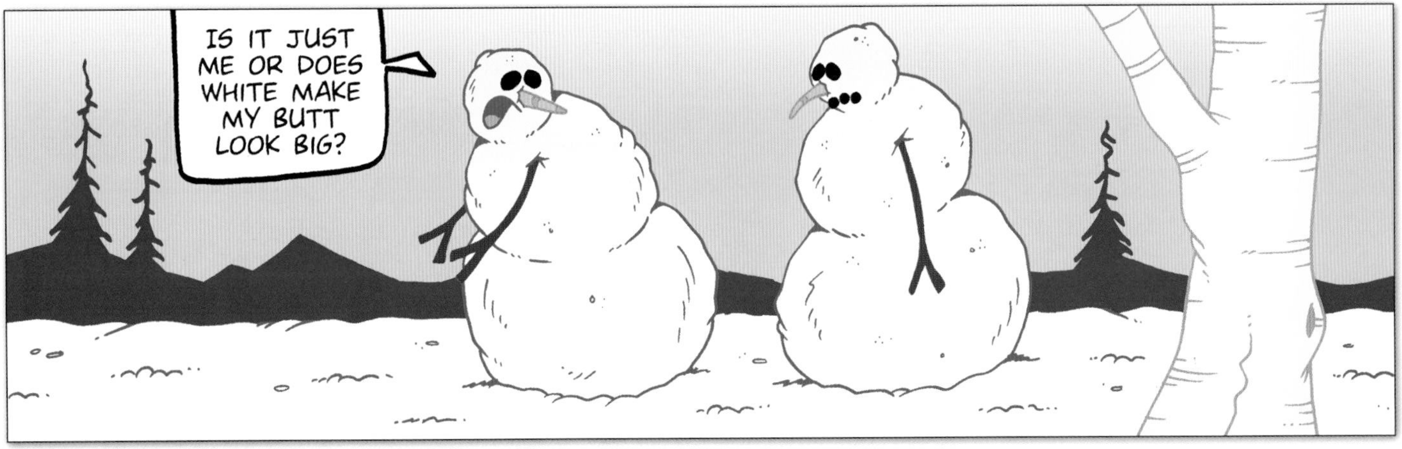
IS IT JUST ME OR DOES WHITE MAKE MY BUTT LOOK BIG?

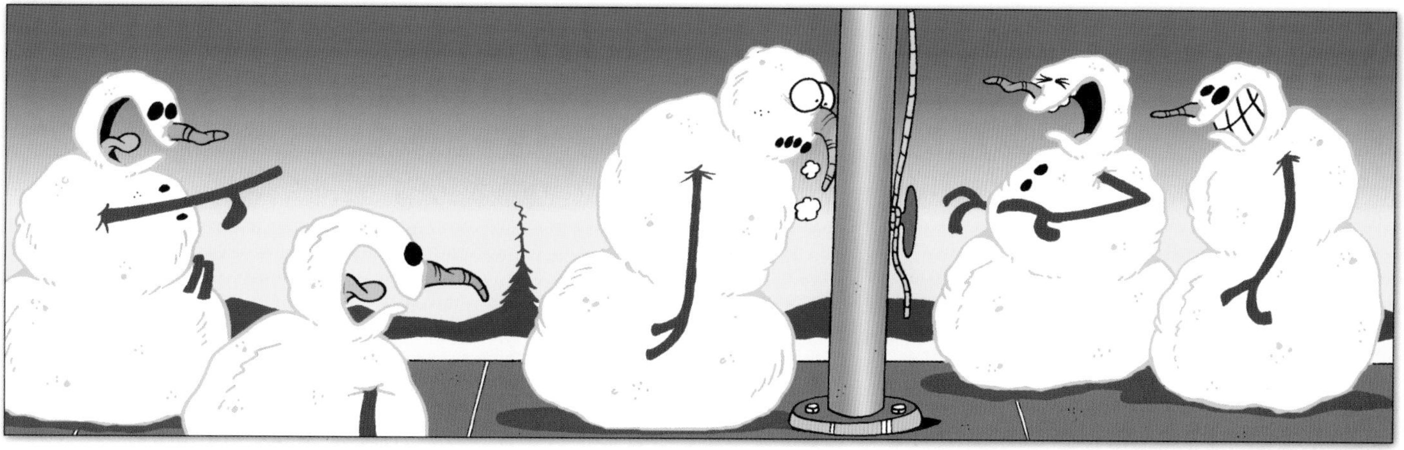

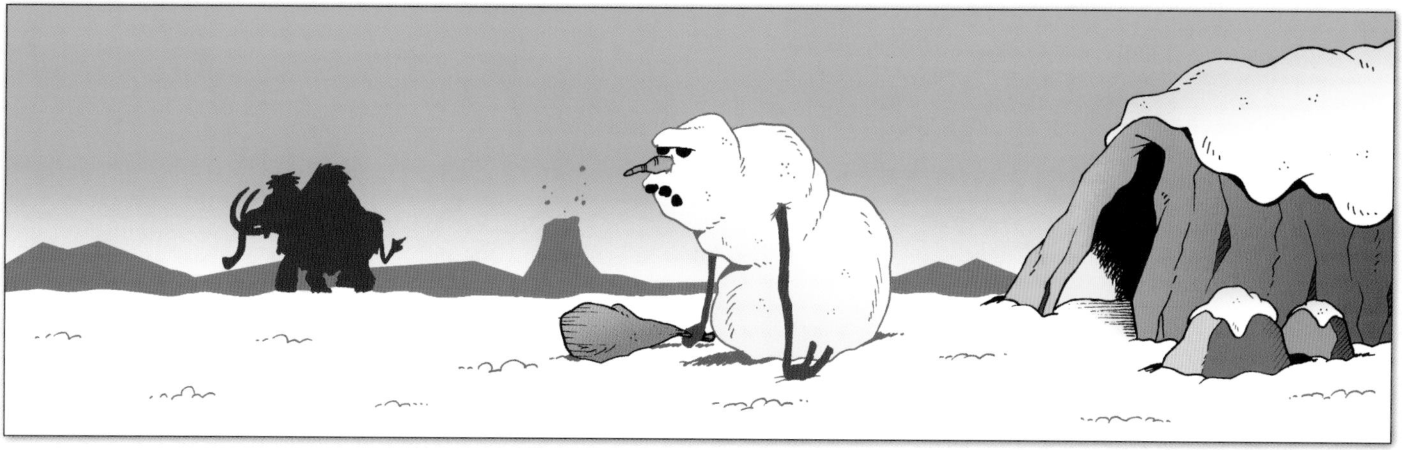

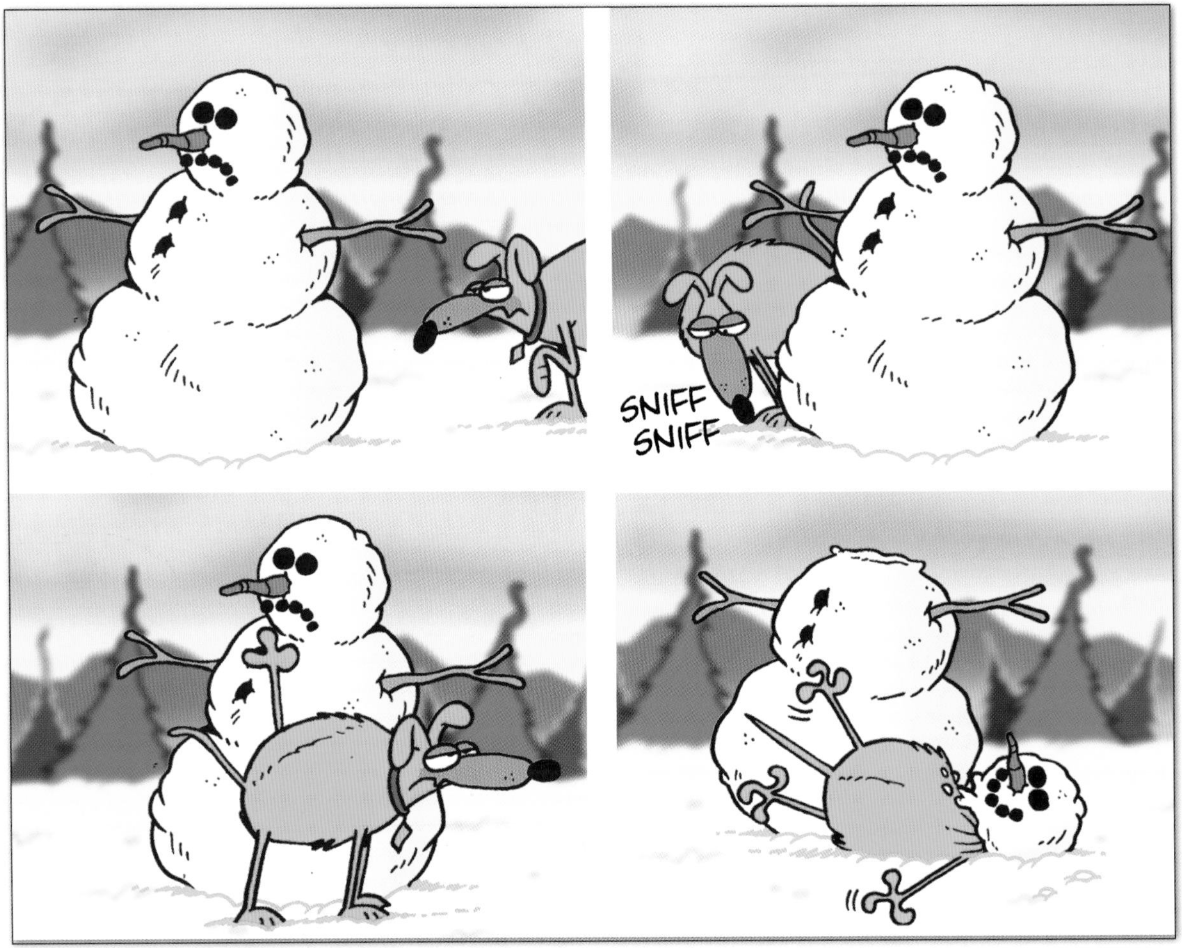
SNIFF
SNIFF

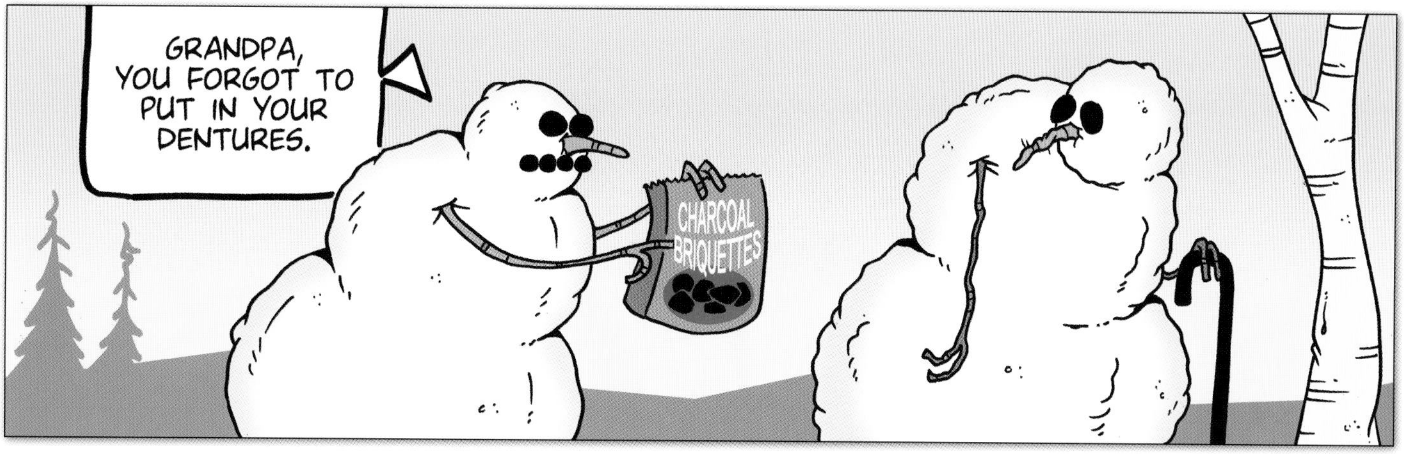
GRANDPA, YOU FORGOT TO PUT IN YOUR DENTURES.
CHARCOAL BRIQUETTES

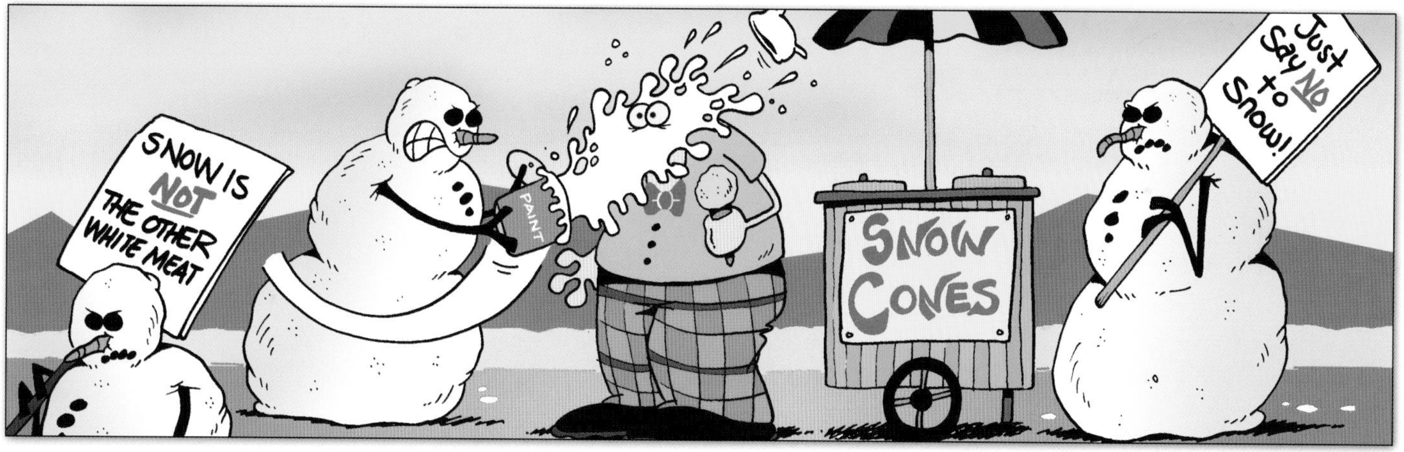
SNOW IS NOT THE OTHER WHITE MEAT
PAINT
SNOW CONES
Just Say NO to Snow!

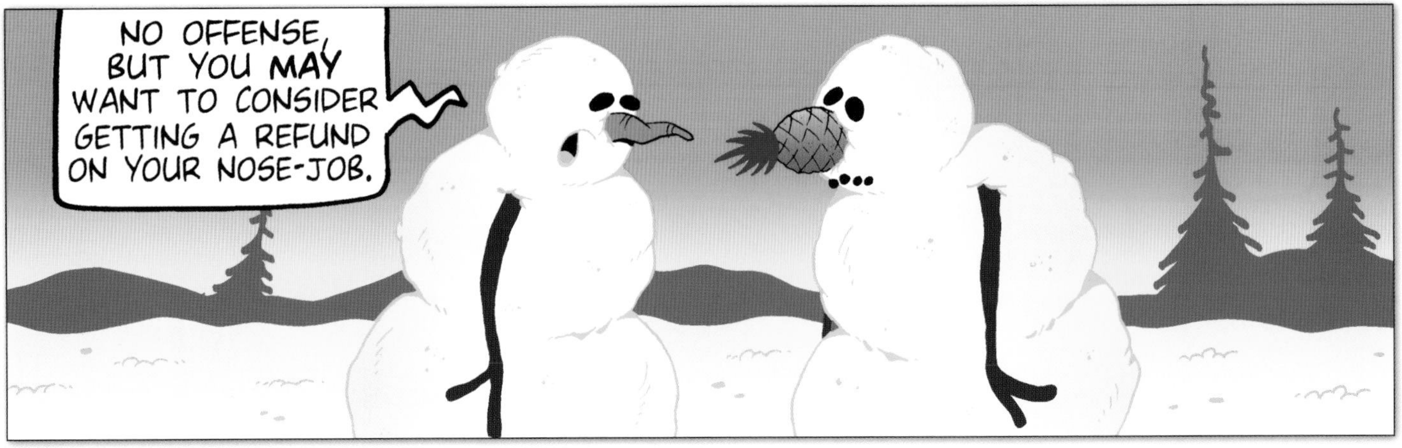
NO OFFENSE, BUT YOU MAY WANT TO CONSIDER GETTING A REFUND ON YOUR NOSE-JOB.

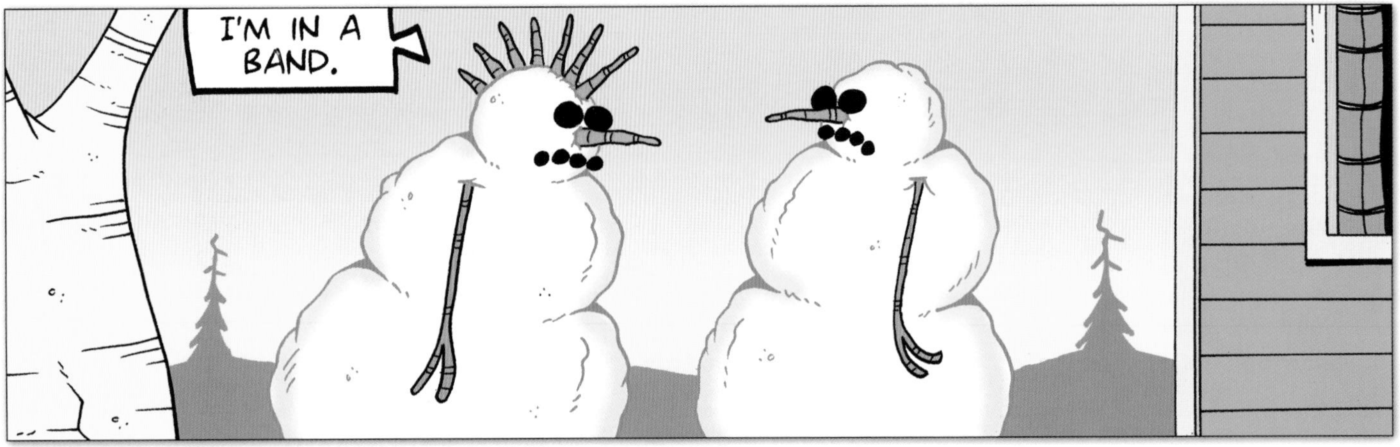
I'M IN A BAND.

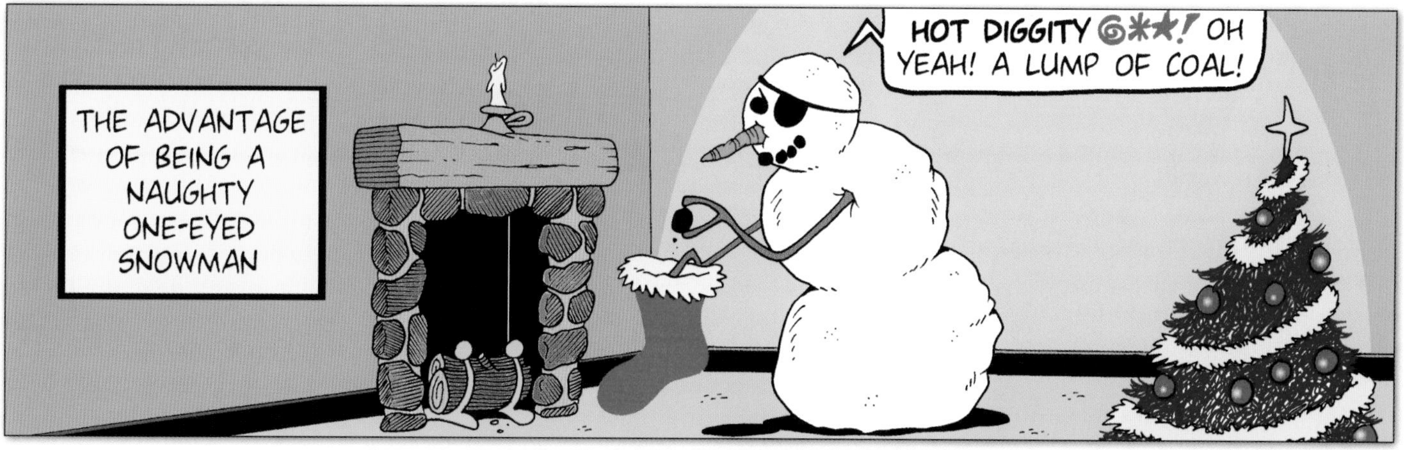
THE ADVANTAGE OF BEING A NAUGHTY ONE-EYED SNOWMAN
HOT DIGGITY @**! OH YEAH! A LUMP OF COAL!

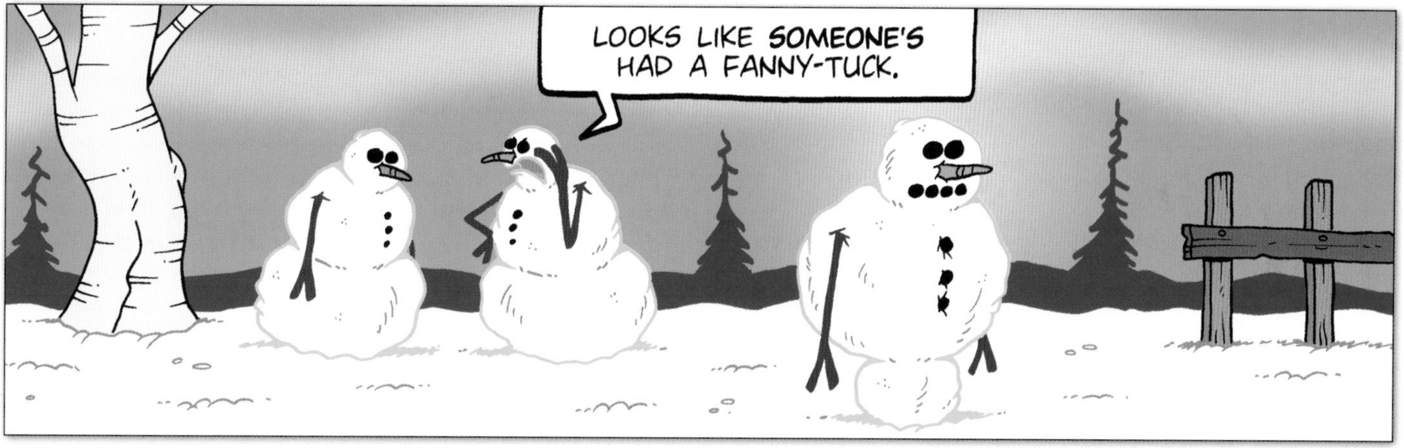
LOOKS LIKE SOMEONE'S HAD A FANNY-TUCK.

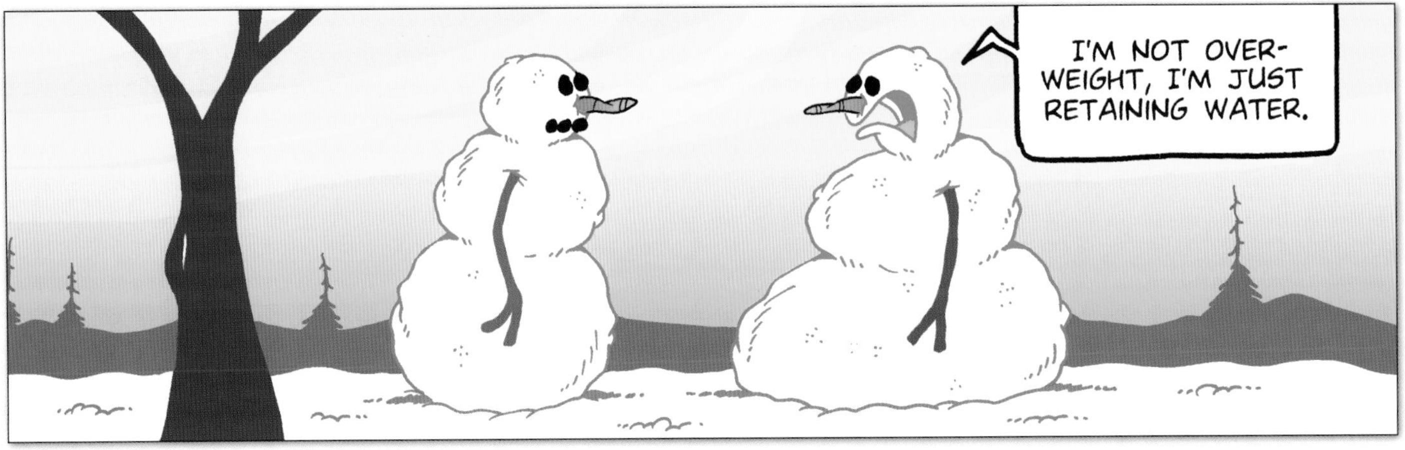
I'M NOT OVER-WEIGHT, I'M JUST RETAINING WATER.

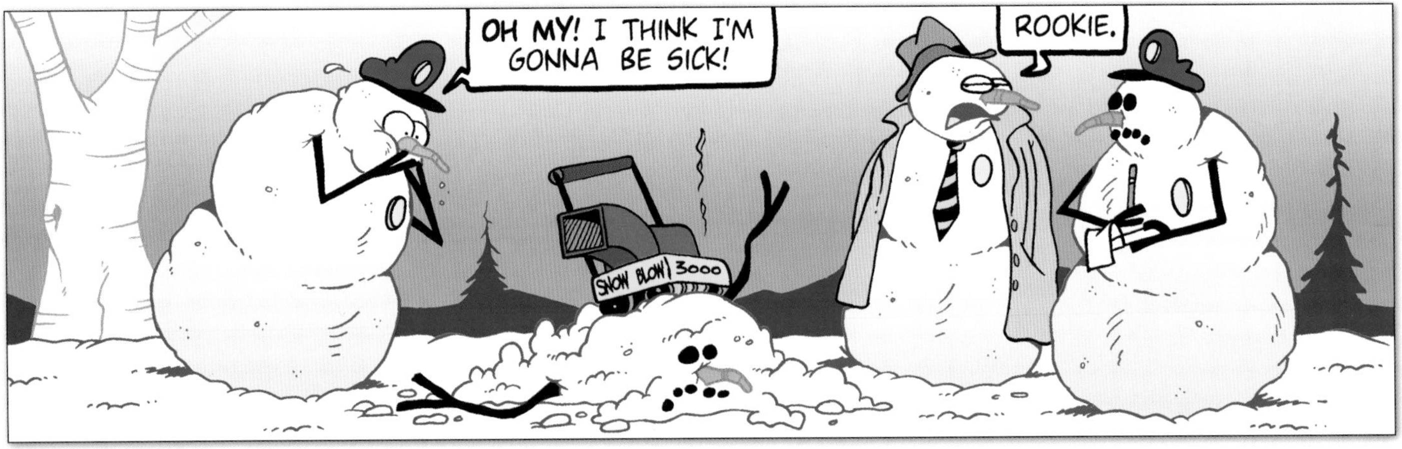
OH MY! I THINK I'M GONNA BE SICK!
SNOW BLOW 3000
ROOKIE.

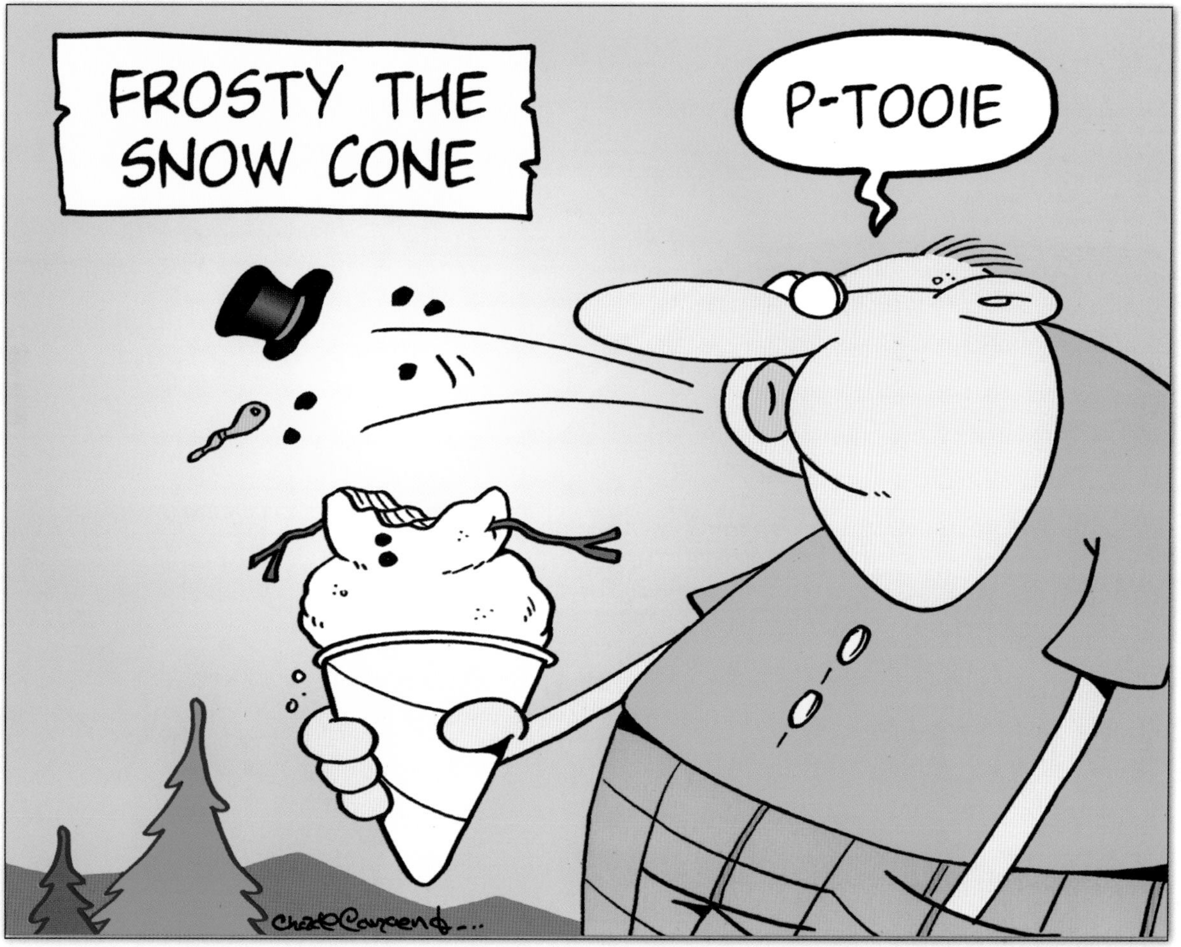
FROSTY THE SNOW CONE
P-TOOIE

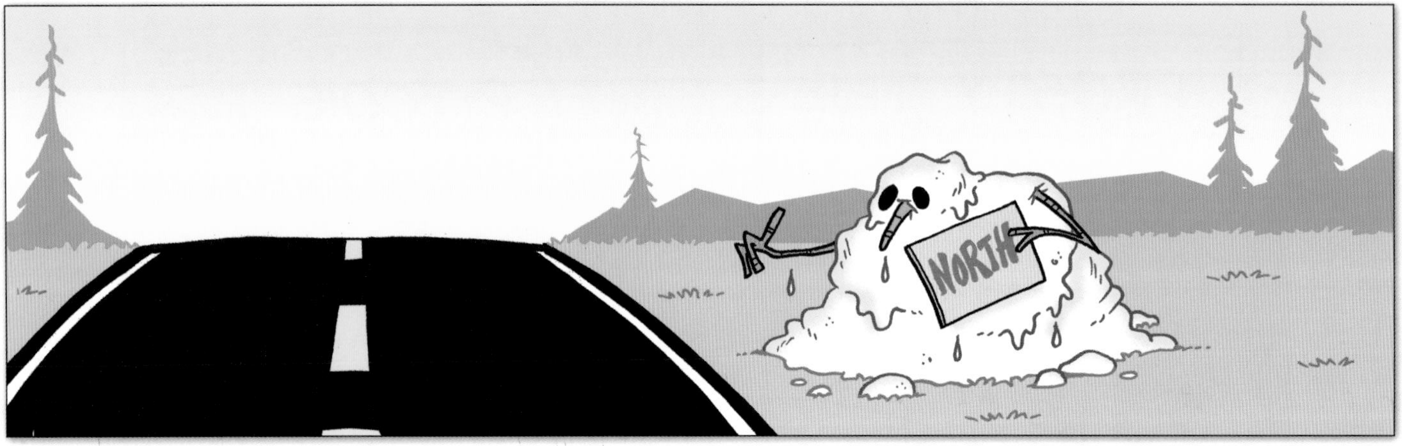
NORTH

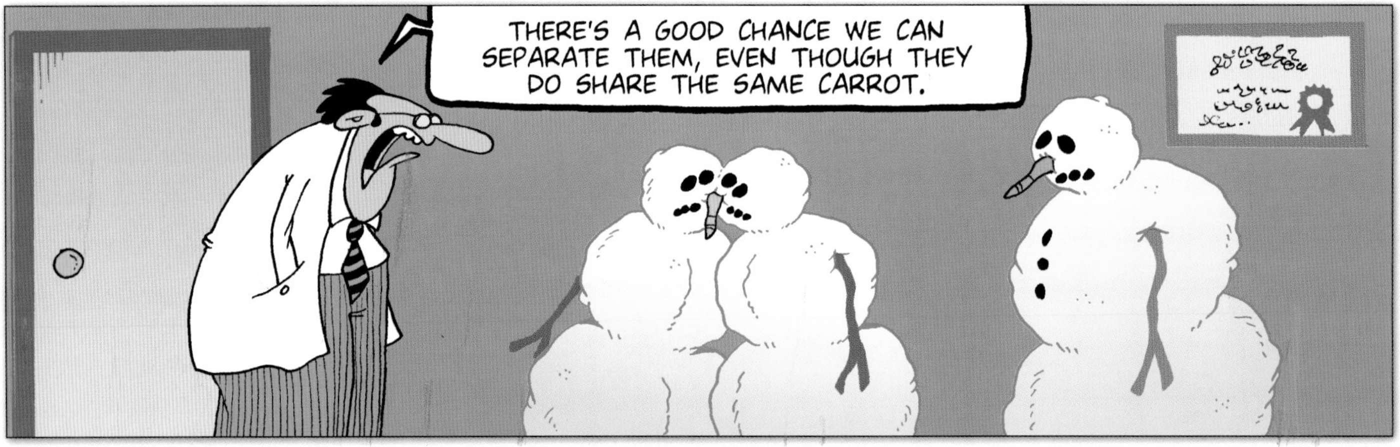
THERE'S A GOOD CHANCE WE CAN SEPARATE THEM, EVEN THOUGH THEY DO SHARE THE SAME CARROT.

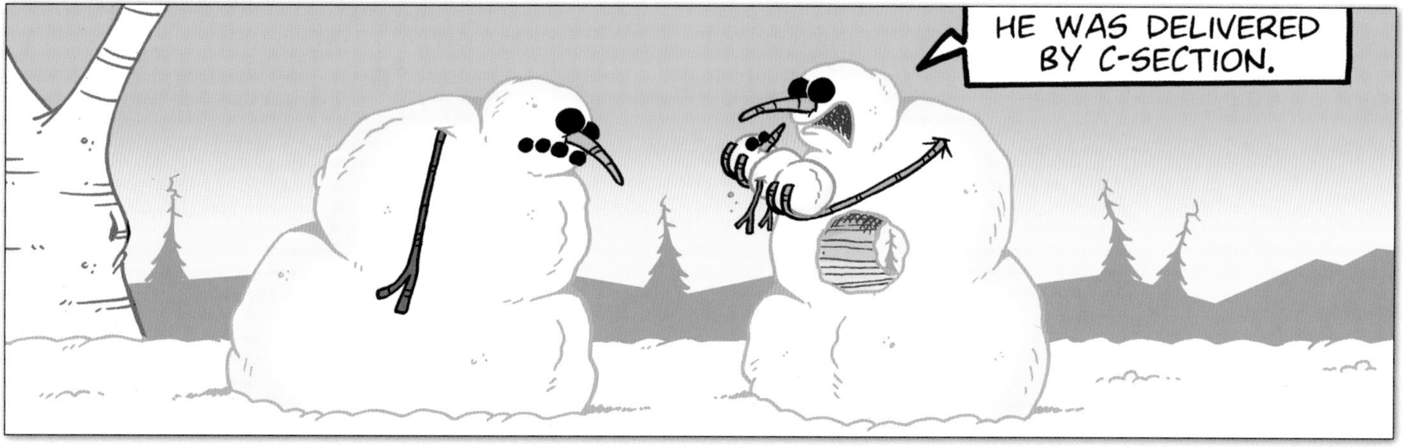
HE WAS DELIVERED BY C-SECTION.

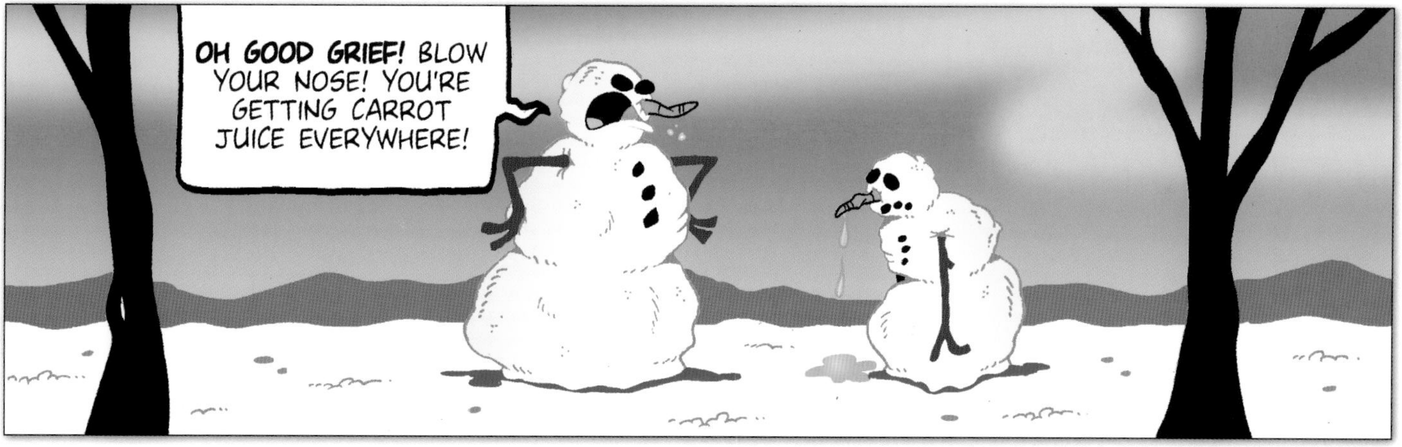
OH GOOD GRIEF! BLOW YOUR NOSE! YOU'RE GETTING CARROT JUICE EVERYWHERE!

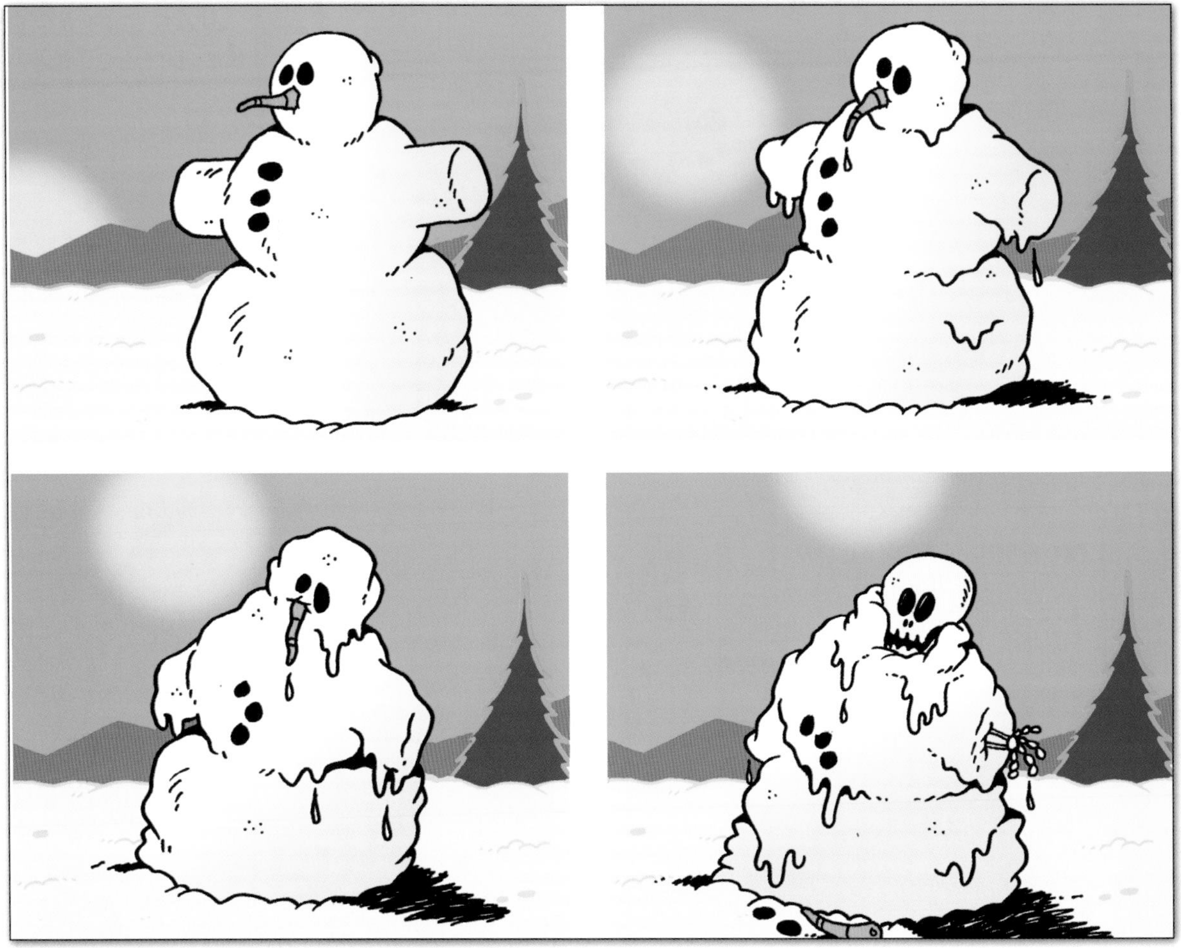

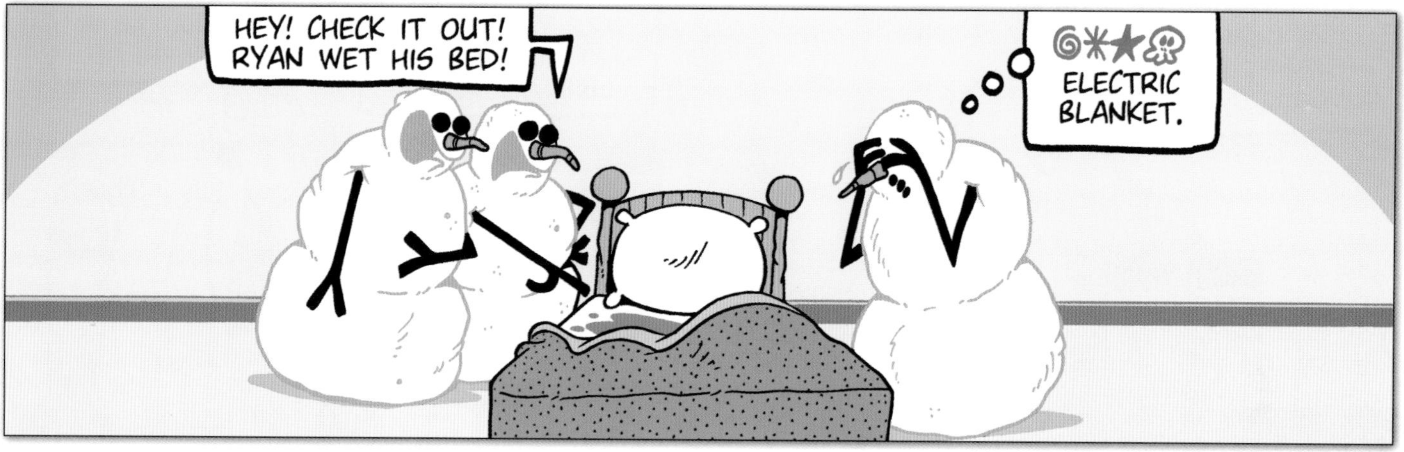
HEY! CHECK IT OUT! RYAN WET HIS BED!
ELECTRIC BLANKET.

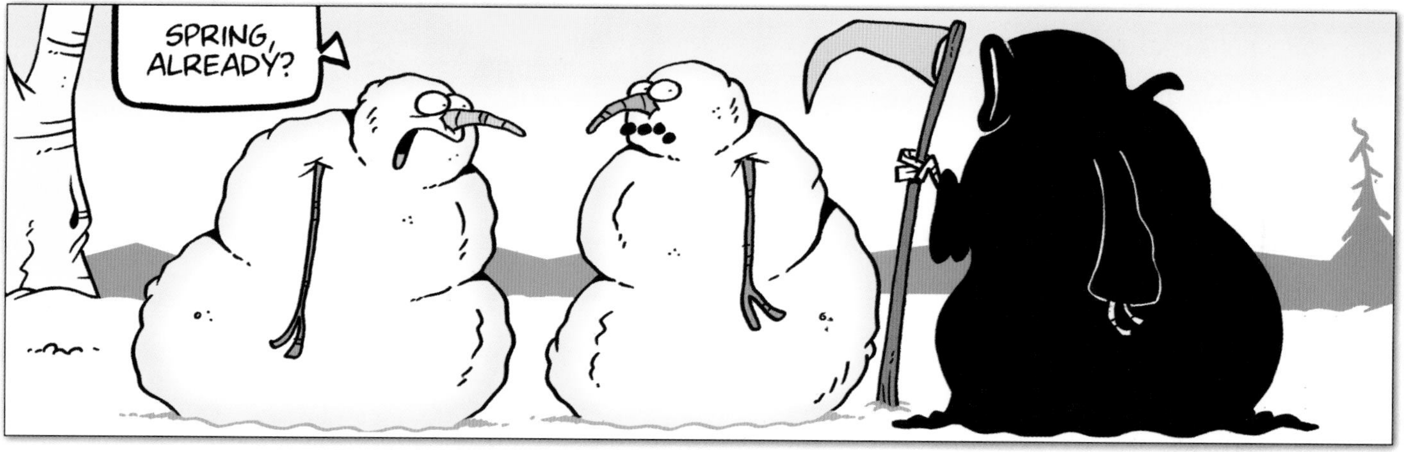
SPRING, ALREADY?

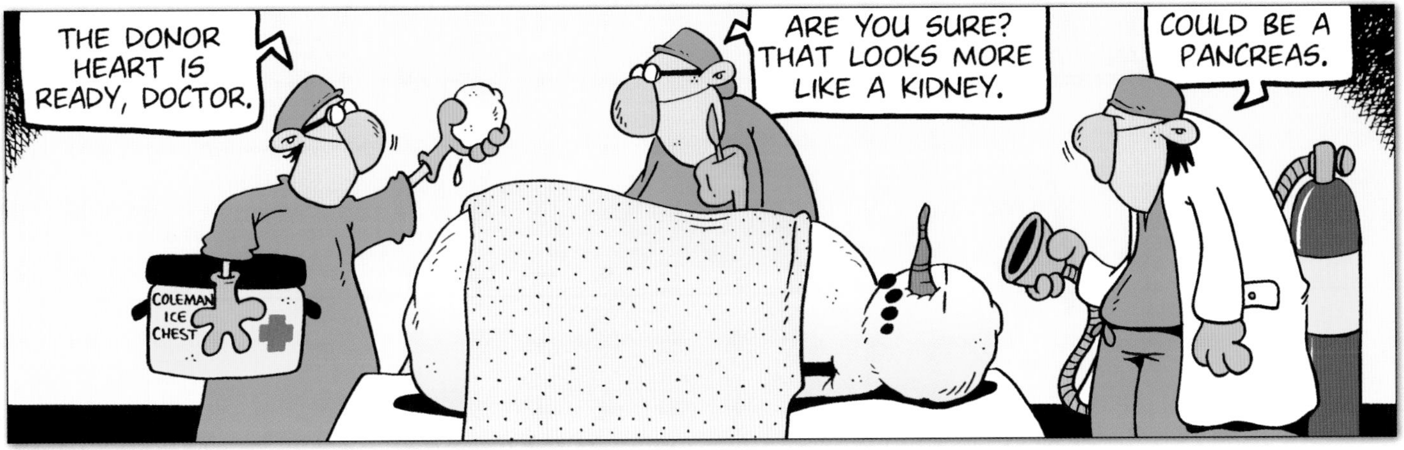
THE DONOR HEART IS READY, DOCTOR.
ARE YOU SURE? THAT LOOKS MORE LIKE A KIDNEY.
COULD BE A PANCREAS.
COLEMAN ICE CHEST

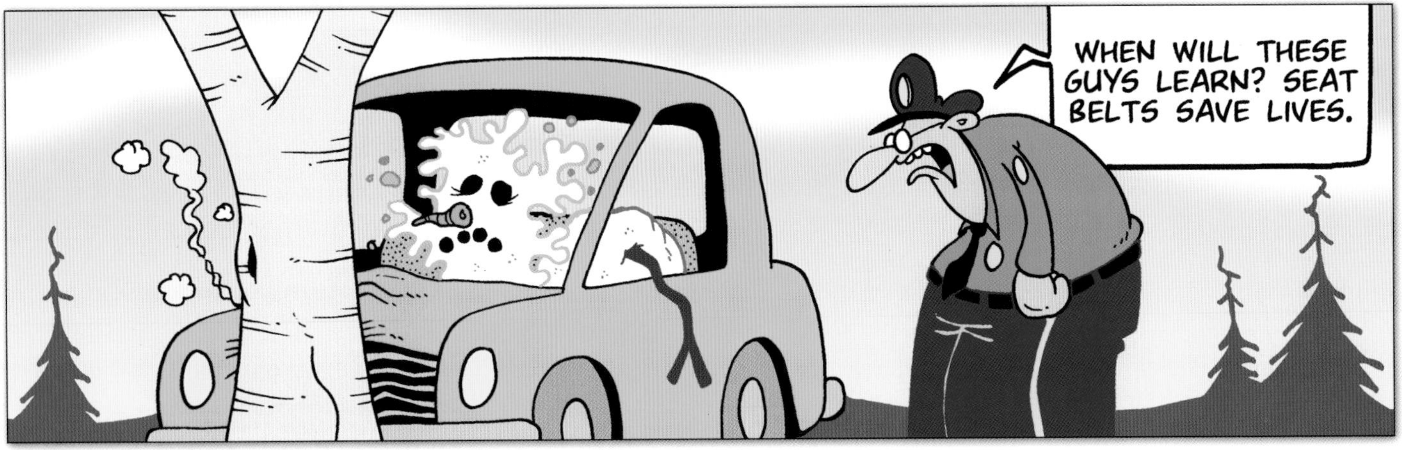
WHEN WILL THESE GUYS LEARN? SEAT BELTS SAVE LIVES.

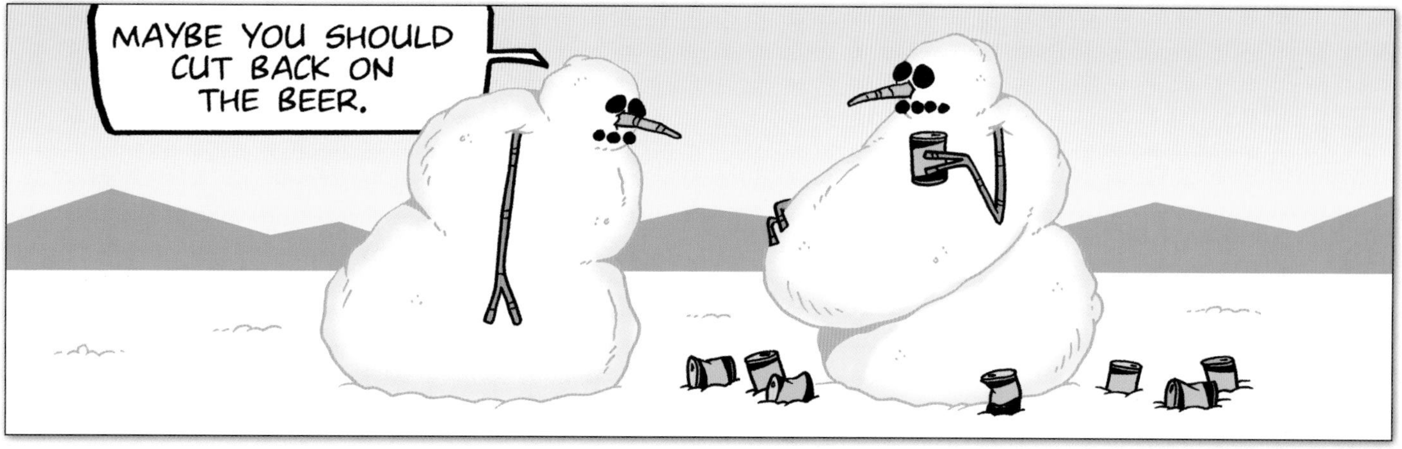
MAYBE YOU SHOULD CUT BACK ON THE BEER.

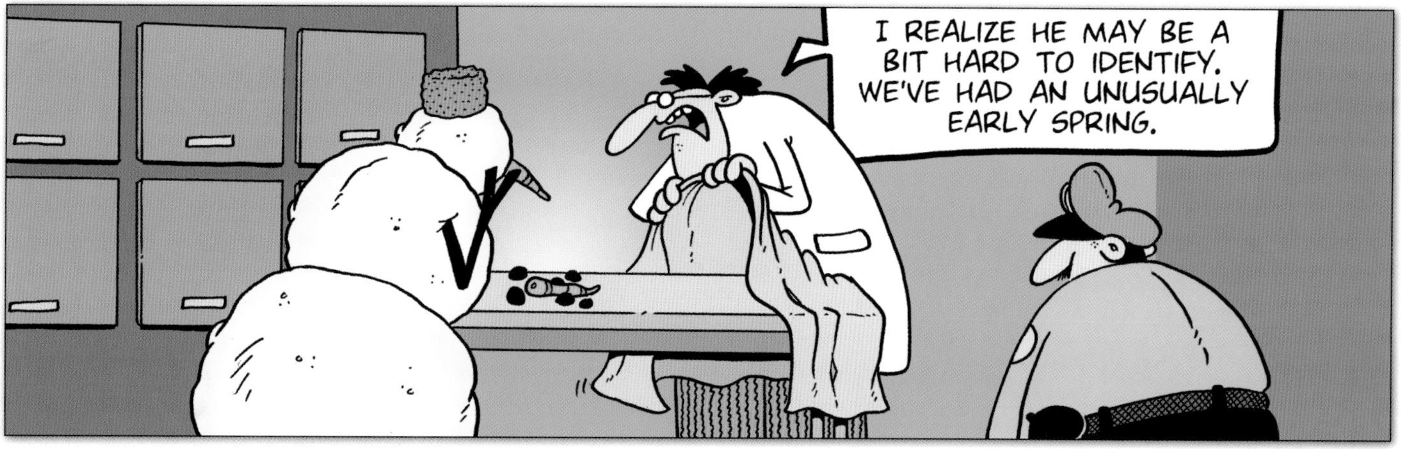
I REALIZE HE MAY BE A BIT HARD TO IDENTIFY. WE'VE HAD AN UNUSUALLY EARLY SPRING.

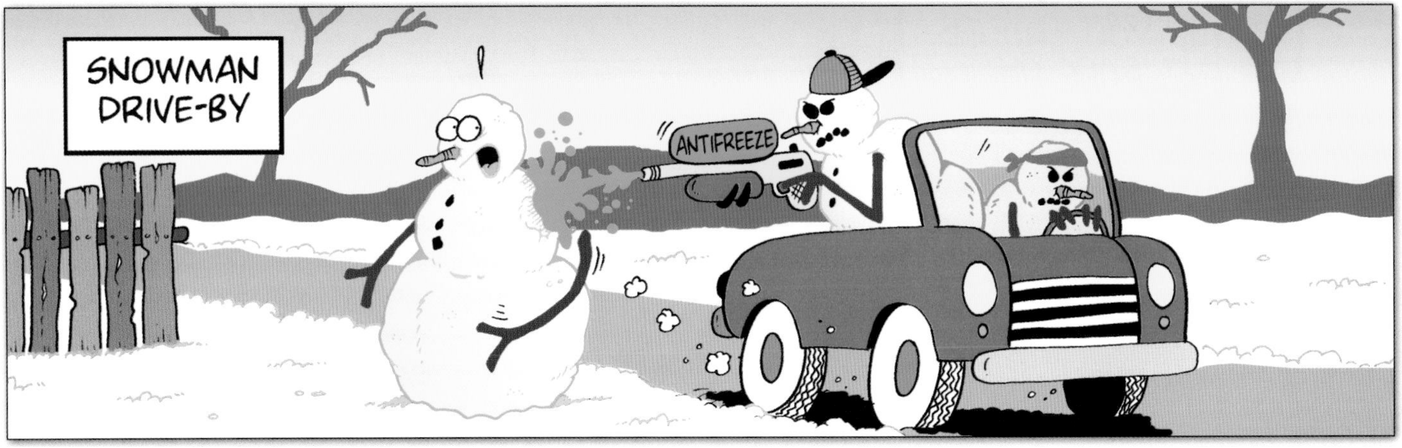
SNOWMAN
DRIVE-BY
ANTIFREEZE

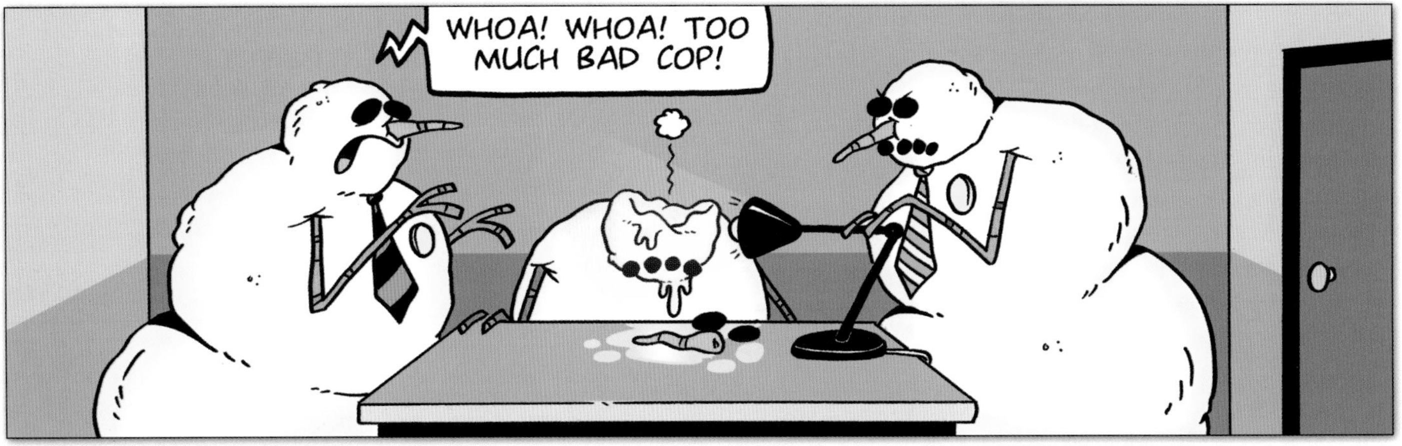
WHOA! WHOA! TOO
MUCH BAD COP!

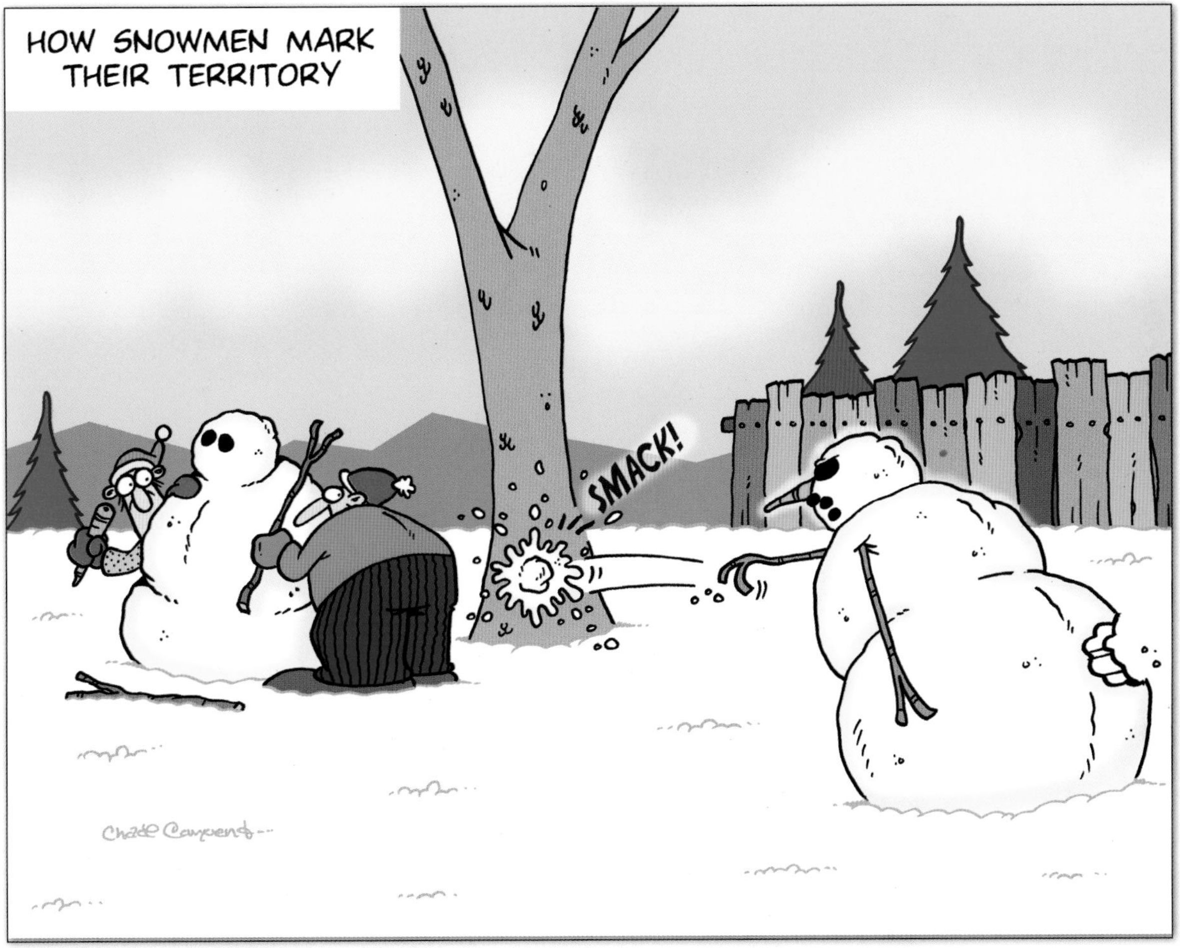
HOW SNOWMEN MARK THEIR TERRITORY
SMACK!

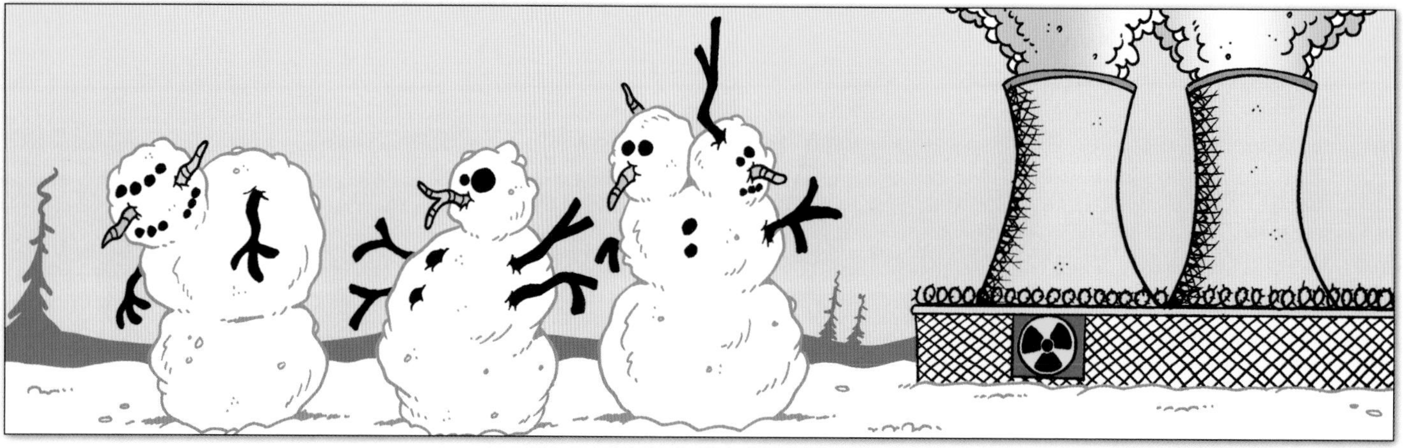

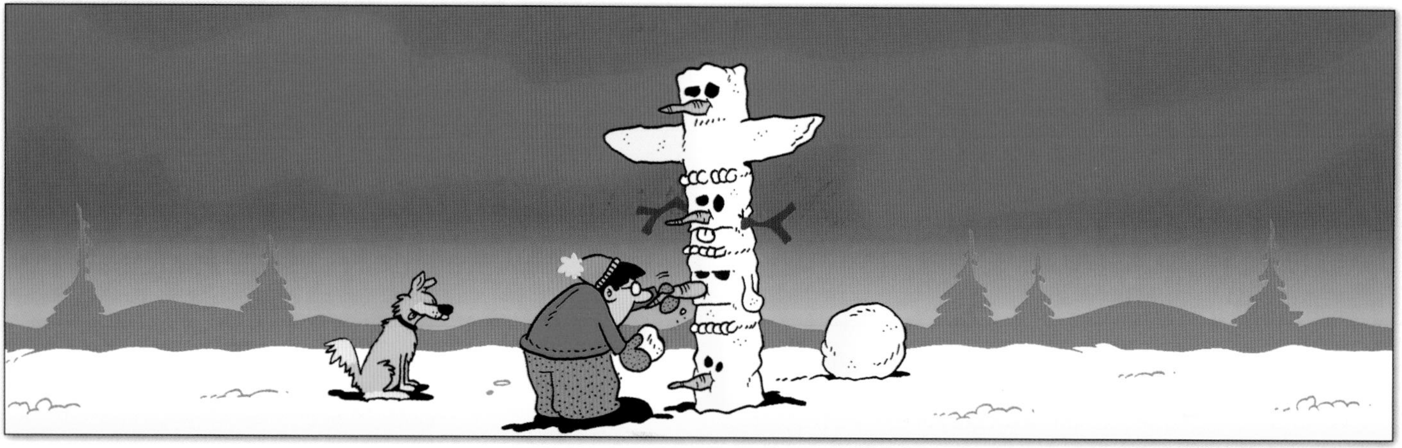

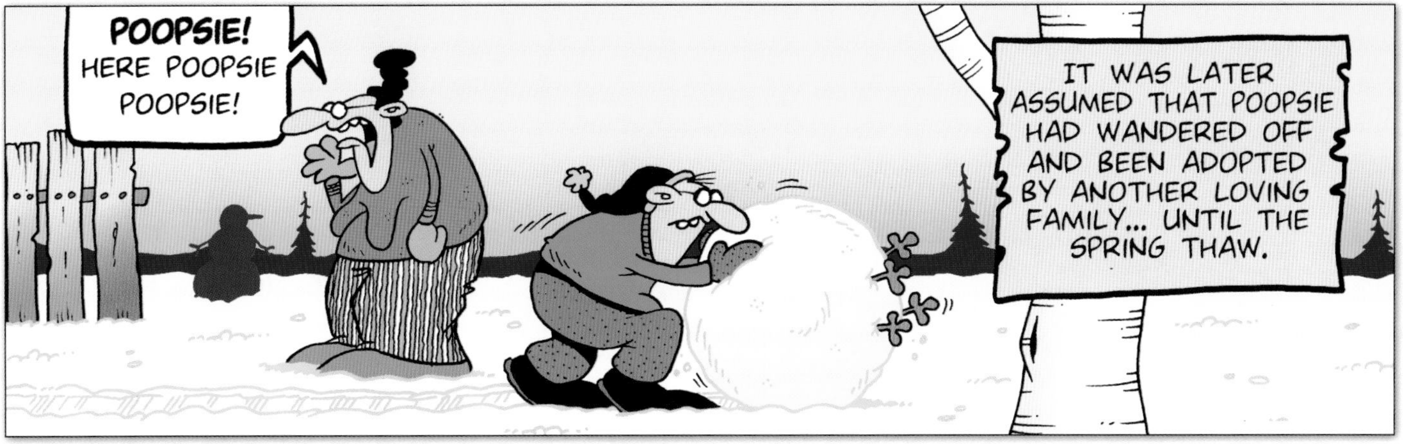
POOPSIE!
HERE POOPSIE POOPSIE!
IT WAS LATER ASSUMED THAT POOPSIE HAD WANDERED OFF AND BEEN ADOPTED BY ANOTHER LOVING FAMILY... UNTIL THE SPRING THAW.

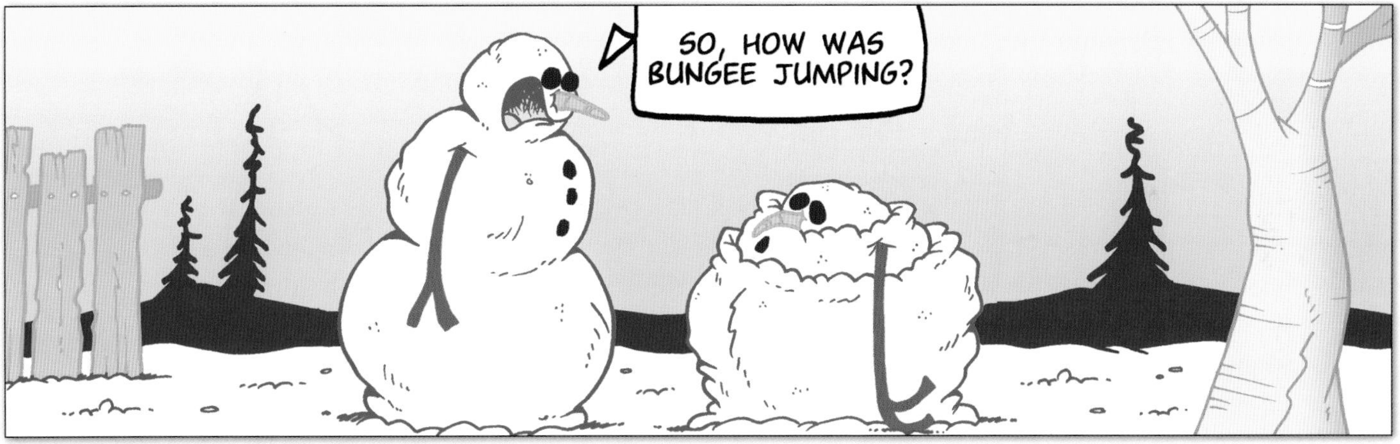
SO, HOW WAS BUNGEE JUMPING?

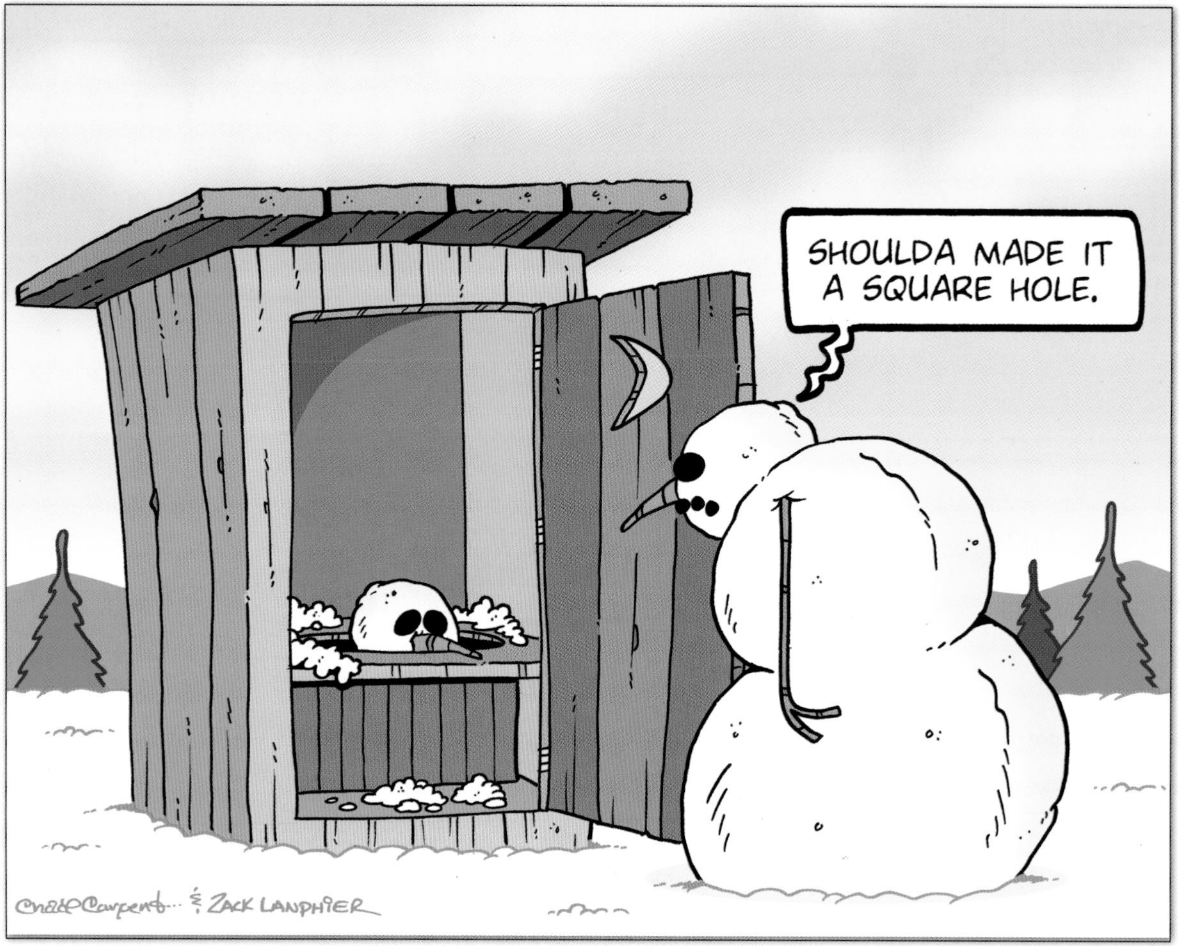
SHOULDA MADE IT A SQUARE HOLE.
©Dave Carpenter & ZACK LANPHIER

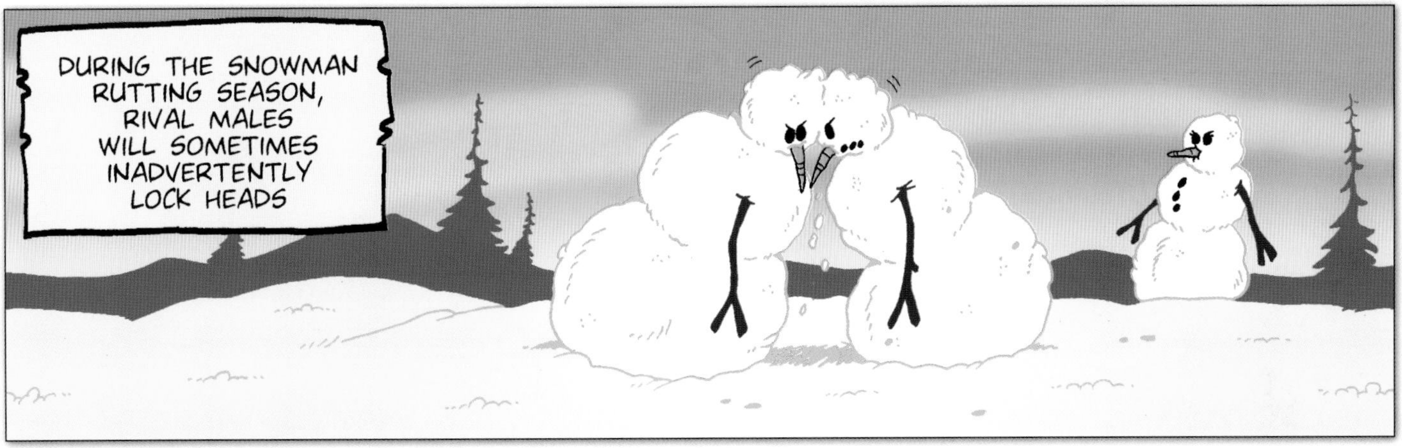
DURING THE SNOWMAN RUTTING SEASON, RIVAL MALES WILL SOMETIMES INADVERTENTLY LOCK HEADS

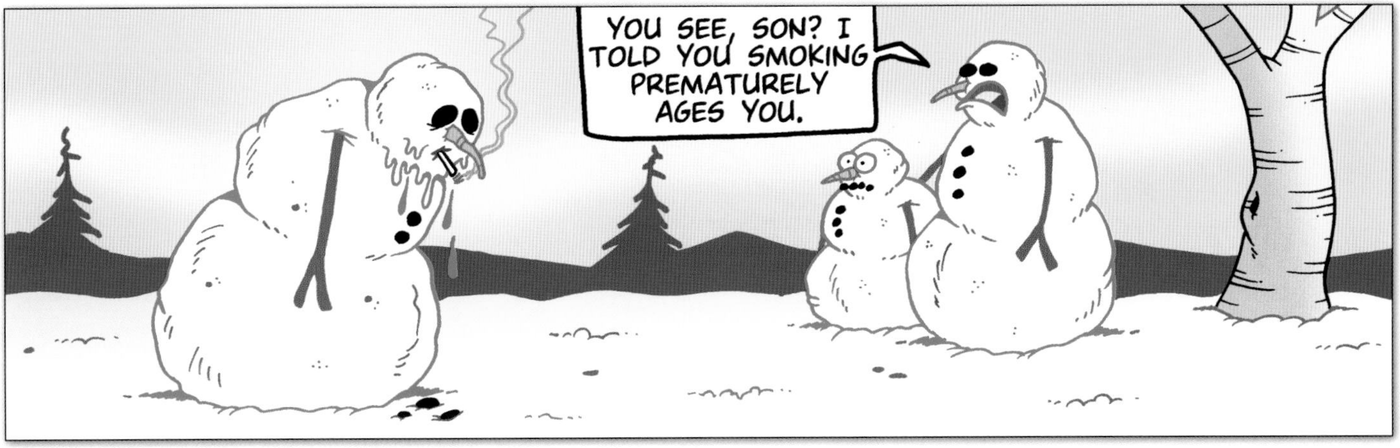
YOU SEE, SON? I TOLD YOU SMOKING PREMATURELY AGES YOU.

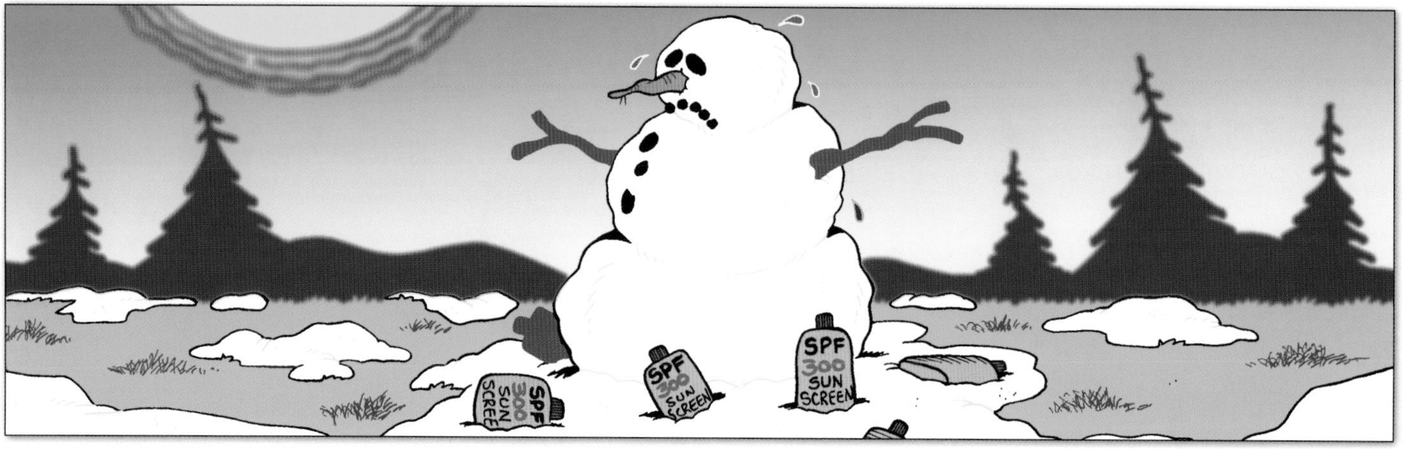
SPF 300 SUN SCREEN
SPF 300 SUN SCREEN
SPF 300 SUN SCREE

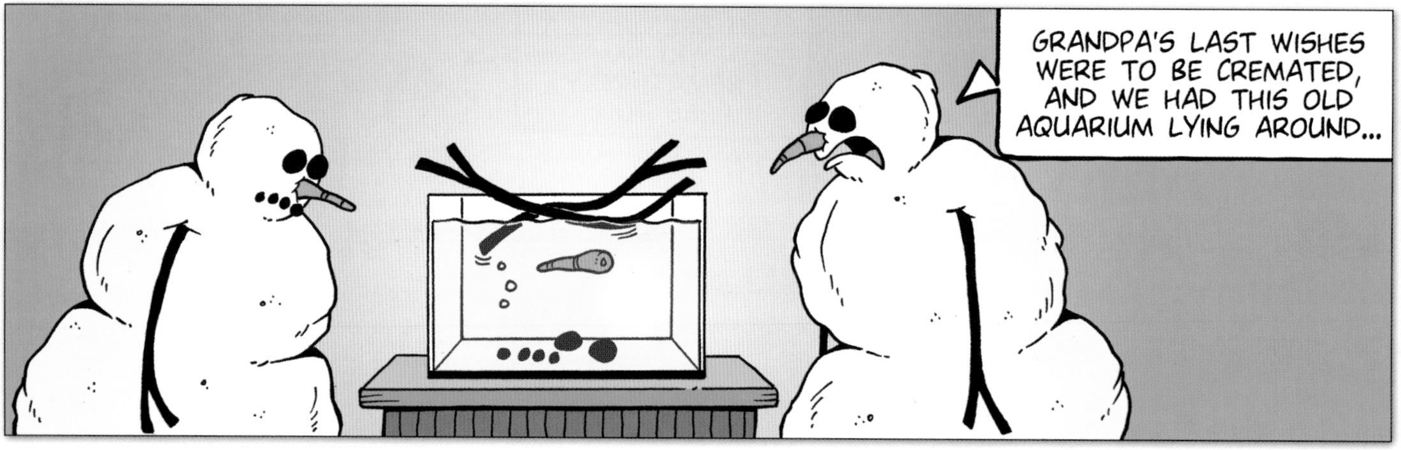
GRANDPA'S LAST WISHES WERE TO BE CREMATED, AND WE HAD THIS OLD AQUARIUM LYING AROUND...

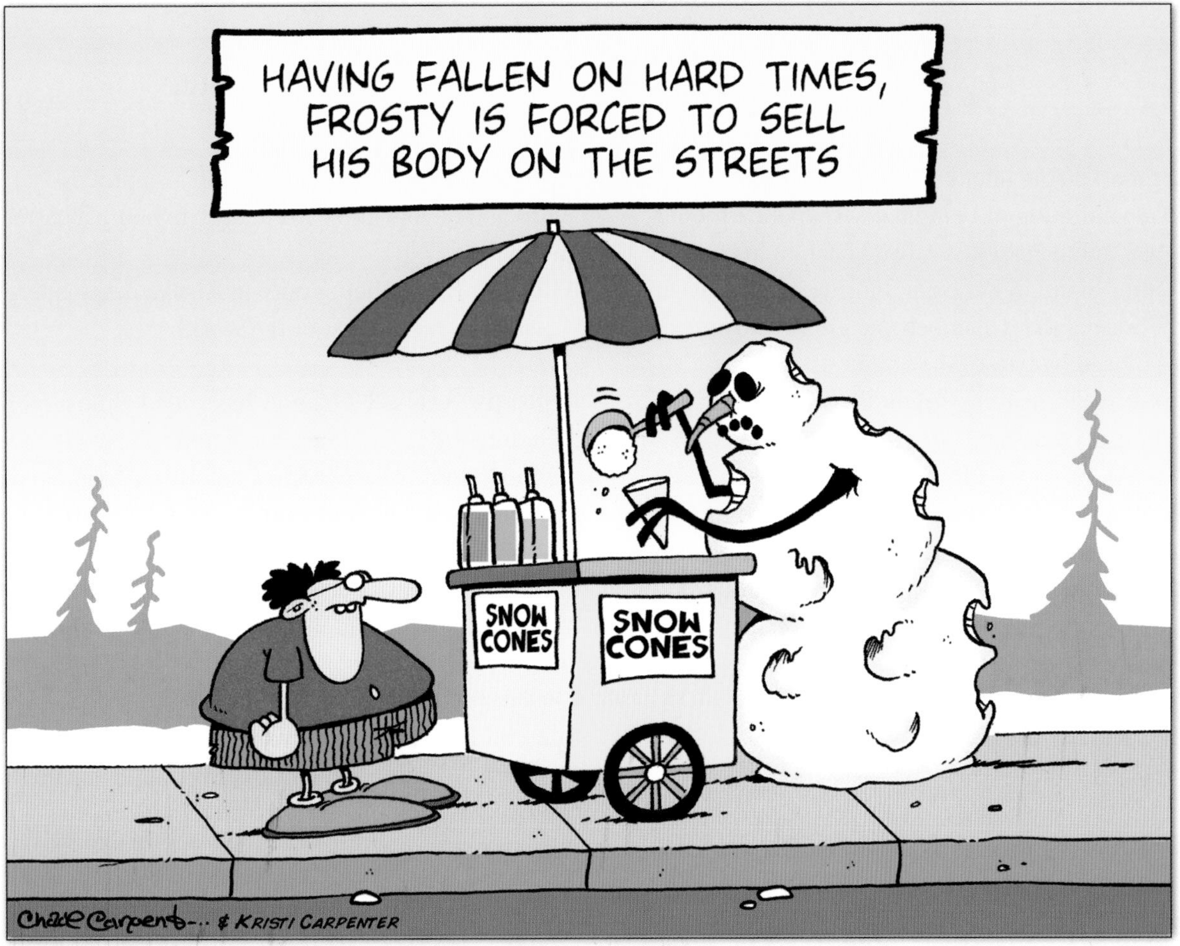
HAVING FALLEN ON HARD TIMES, FROSTY IS FORCED TO SELL HIS BODY ON THE STREETS
SNOW CONES
SNOW CONES
Chad Carpenter... & KRISTI CARPENTER

The Official Short but Sweet Bio of Chad Carpenter

Having no other marketable talent, Chad decided to take a crack at a life-long ambition of being a newspaper cartoonist. The year was 1991 and he had just moved back to his home state of Alaska after living in Sarasota, Florida for three years. It was while in Sarasota that Chad became greatly inspired and personally advised by two of the comic strip greats - Mike Peters (Mother Goose & Grimm) & Dik Browne (Hagar the Horrible).

Shortly After arriving back in Alaska, armed with little more than 36 sample strips, a whole lot of ignorance and a burning desire to avoid real work, Chad went to the Anchorage Daily News to pedal his wares. The features editor took one look at "Tundra" and said "Eh, maybe we'll give it a try."

Fortunately, they actually did.

Shortly after the Daily News started running TUNDRA, it was picked up by most of the other Alaskan newspapers. A year later Chad was able to quit his job as a process server/security guard and devote all of his energy to being a cartoonist.

After 15 years of being only in Alaska newspapers, TUNDRA broke loose on the rest of the world.

In just five years, TUNDRA has added almost 500 newspapers including the L.A. Times, the Seattle Times, the Denver Post, the Pittsburgh Post, the San Francisco Chronicle as well as newspapers throughout Europe, Jamaica & Trinidad.

In May of 2008 Chad was presented with the Reuben Award for "Best Newspaper Panel" by the National Cartoonist Society.

Chad currently lives in Wasilla, Alaska with his wife Karen and four children. He is busy working on his 21st book as well as the latest calendars, shirts, greeting cards and anything else he can make a buck on.